SYSTEMIC WORK
WITH ORGANIZATIONS

Other titles in the

Systemic Thinking and Practice Series

edited by David Campbell & Ros Draper
published and distributed by Karnac Books

Credit Card orders, Tel: 071-584-3303; Fax: 071-823-7743

SYSTEMIC WORK WITH ORGANIZATIONS

A New Model for Managers and Change Agents

David Campbell
Tim Coldicott
Keith Kinsella

Systemic Thinking and Practice Series
Work with Organizations

Series Editors
David Campbell & Ros Draper

London
KARNAC BOOKS

This edition first published in 1994 by
H. Karnac (Books) Ltd.
58 Gloucester Road
London SW7 4QY

British Library Cataloguing in Publication Data

Campbell, David
    Systemic Work with Organizations: A New
    Model for Managers and Change Agents. —
    (Systemic Thinking & Practice Series)
    I. Title II. Series
    658

    ISBN 1 85575 100 3

Printed in Great Britain by BPC Wheatons Ltd, Exeter

CONTENTS

PART ONE
Approach—
adapting theory to a new context

EDITORS' FOREWORD

One of the unique features of this book is the fact that the three authors, from very diverse backgrounds, have come together at this particular time to create a conjoint approach to work with organizations. From psychology and commerce and engineering they have reached a common commitment to a new way of understanding organizations. They are transposing systemic thinking from its origins in the therapeutic and academic world of the social sciences to the hard-edged world of organizational life. For years it has seemed eminently logical to think of organizations as systems, but no one has devised a method for using these ideas to bring about change. Because the authors are amongst only a handful who are applying these new ideas as consultants to a range of public and private sector organizations, they are preoccupied with the problem of understanding and evaluating their own work: "What works in which situation . . . and what doesn't work . . . and why?" Their aim is to gather their experiences together into a methodology that will enable other practitioners to use these ideas.

Why should this book be appropriate at this particular time? As editors we believe that the ideas in the book mirror the increasing complexity of life today and the need to acknowledge an increasing range of views and opinions about any issue. The days of simple structures and easy explanations are gone, and practitioners need tools to help them make sense of this emerging diversity. We see systemic thinking—and its application called constructionist consultancy—as just such tools.

We are also aware that this book introduces this Series to a new market. It aspires to create new ground—between the social scientists and organization change agents—where new thinking can be applied to old problems and where old ways of thinking can be challenged with new techniques. The authors wrote with a new audience in mind because they believe that increasingly complicated organizational problems require a different kind of practitioner than has existed before. They have tried to make the book and its ideas as accessible and concise as possible, knowing full well that some people find the language of systems thinking very strange, and that managers and consultants do not have time to wade through lengthy tomes to garner fresh ideas.

We hope familiar readers will find systemic ideas placed in new contexts; for those of you coming to this field for the first time, welcome!

David Campbell
Ros Draper

London
October 1994

SYSTEMIC WORK WITH ORGANIZATIONS

Introduction

T his book is written for managers, consultants, or people aspiring to become consultants—for those, such as human resources staff, with responsibility for managing change within their own organization, or those who have reached a position of long experience in their own field and are now changing their role to consult to others.

The authors' experience spans the public and private sectors. The ideas in this book have been useful in the fields of health, education, and local authority government, as well as in commerce and industry. We have found among our public sector clients growing acceptance of the need today to import ideas from the private sector, but at the same time a concern among these managers that they do not have a context that gives meaning to the imported ideas. The counterflow into the private sector of ideas about collaboration, governance, ethics, and support for community has presented similar problems. It is this difficulty of helping clients translate and fit knowledge and practice from one sphere of action to another that has provided a central challenge to the authors as they have developed their model of systemic working.

To grapple more effectively with a world of work in which there is an increasing fragmentation of traditional structures and values, the authors put forward two central ideas:

1. when people think systemically, they are able to understand better the effects of connectedness in organizations, and account more effectively for the dilemmas and tensions that arise during change;

2. when people understand and accept how they collectively create and maintain mental pictures of the organization and its problems, they are able to alter and renegotiate these understandings and find new ways of solving their problems.

Although many consultancy techniques are presented here, this is not just a book of techniques. The authors describe a way of thinking, a way of being, as a systemic consultant that is akin to developing a new identity. From this new position, a consultant negotiates the work with clients and creates techniques to address the demands of a consultation process in a way that is different from and, we believe, more productive than traditional consultancy services.

We are convinced that one does not become a systemic thinker or a constructionist consultant by reading. This book is not a manual telling the reader "how to do it". Rather, it is an introduction to the ideas and practices that the authors have found successful and compelling; readers will have to go much further before applying these ideas to their own practice. We have found the best way to progress is to work with other people who share an interest in developing systemic ideas.

The work in this volume will be described with a particular terminology which may be new for some readers, and for this reason a comprehensive glossary is included at the end of the book. However, two terms in particular should be clarified at the outset:

1. *Systemic* refers to the broad field of ideas derived from General Systems Theory and expanded in several directions since the 1960s. These ideas will become clear and familiar as the reader proceeds through the book.

2. *Constructionist* refers to some aspects of systemic thinking that focus on the construction of problems in organizations and the

attention a consultant pays to addressing that construction and to facilitating the client towards new constructions. Although based on systemic thinking, we have coined the term *constructionist consulting* to distinguish this type of consultancy from more traditional expert or process models.

Many readers will be aware of the new meaning of the word "systemic": for decades it has been a central concept describing integrated operational systems in the computing and engineering fields, and those of you who are avid gardeners feed your roses with "systemic" fertilizers. However, there is a new generation of systemic ideas which has been introduced to organizational thinking primarily through a different route—human systems. Historically, these ideas from the computer revolution of the 1950s and 1960s were first applied to human systems by practitioners who were working with whole families. The idea of seeing the family as an interrelated system that creates a collective meaning for individual behaviours has proved profoundly helpful to those who are trying to understand complex problems such as mental illness, alcoholism, or marital breakdown. As a result, an approach to human problems based on "systemic thinking" emerged in the 1960s and has continuously expanded and been applied to a wide range of behaviours that require new solutions. Readers interested in the historical roots of this approach will enjoy some of the seminal texts, such as Watzlawick, Beavin, and Jackson (1967), Bateson (1973), and Watzlawick, Weakland, and Fisch (1974). For many of these practitioners, it was then only a small step to think of the organization as an interconnected system, and to incorporate these ideas into their work as consultants.

* * *

The book divides into three sections.

Part I, consisting of Chapters 1 and 2, clarifies the conceptual tools that underpin this new approach to consultancy:

• Chapter 1 explains the main concepts adapted from General Systems Theory and developed into the broader framework known as systemic thinking. Each of the concepts forms the basis for some aspect of the consultancy work elaborated throughout the book.

- Chapter 2 is about the way we apply the systemic concepts to the daily practice of consultancy. Familiar topics such as leadership, communication, and change management are discussed and reframed using systemic thinking.

Part II provides three examples of the way systemic ideas have been fashioned into the practice of what the authors call "constructionist consulting":

- Chapter 3 describes how systemic principles were used to design a one-day consultation to a new hospital Trust Board. The focus is on defining the problem and planning a structured consultation to make an impact within a brief period of time.

- Chapter 4 describes a consultation lasting over a four-month period. Here the emphasis is on developing new hypotheses and interventions as the consultant learns more about the organization with each ensuing visit.

- Chapter 5 addresses the implementation of a change programme in a large commercial organization. This study goes beyond planning and strategic thinking to examine new ways to ensure that change works its way through a whole organization.

In each of these real-life cases, the names, locations, and other particular facts have been altered to ensure that the participating organizations cannot be identified.

Part III consolidates the ideas and the practices that have come before and presents ideas for creating a method of work, becoming a constructionist practitioner, and finding work:

- Chapter 6 presents the methodology for using the constructionist model of consultancy as it has emerged from the interplay of concepts and the practice described in the case studies. It is intended as a guide to putting theory into practice and outlines a consulting stance and methodology that we have found successful.

- Chapter 7 describes the process of becoming a constructionist practitioner and creating a distinctive working relationship with clients. We have found ways of renegotiating a consulting role that supports the way we want to work, but also respects the relationship the client expects to have with a consultant.

- Chapter 8 contains descriptions of the personal journeys the authors have taken to arrive at this position of using the constructionist model, the aim being to encourage readers to reflect on their own process of development and perhaps discover ways in which they can also try out some of these ideas.

Although the parts are interconnected, readers who like to begin by knowing who the authors are and how they work as consultants may well begin at the end—with Part III. Others who want to get a practical feel of what the work is like may choose to start with the cases in Part II; whereas those who prefer to establish their conceptual framework before moving on might start at the beginning.

Since the book is written by three authors, we faced the inevitable problem of continuity of ideas and writing styles. However, systemic thinking purports—if nothing else—that we must consider "reality" to be made up of many realities; therefore it seems more consistent with the message of the book not to homogenize the writing, but to allow each author to express himself in his own style. The reader will see how systemic ideas can be expressed in many different ways.

The tone of the book may seem different to many other volumes on the subject of consultancy. Most consultants are paid to be experts, and this is usually reflected in their writing. Our approach is somewhat different. We do not claim to have the "right" answer or even the "best" answer; our expertise lies in an ability to facilitate others to come to a new understanding of the way problems are constructed and maintained in organizations. This leads to client-based solutions. We are constantly exploring and probing in order to stimulate thinking in others that will help both us and them see things differently—and more clearly. We hope our writing reflects our interest in stimulating thoughts in the readers' minds rather than convincing them of our brilliance.

Finally, we acknowledge that there is an inevitable gender bias due to the fact that the three authors are male. We are aware that we talk of "he" where it could be either "he" or "she" but in the interests of readability decided against repeatedly saying "s/he" instead. We hope that male and female readers equally find the book approachable and relevant to their own work.

PART I

APPROACH— ADAPTING THEORY TO A NEW CONTEXT

"It is the theory which decides what we can observe."

Albert Einstein

"There's nothing so practical as a good theory . . ."

Anon.

CHAPTER 1

Key concepts
of systemic thinking

The first chapter provides an understanding of the origin and the conceptual framework of systemic thinking. The book as a whole applies these ideas in many different ways, and ultimately they form the basis for a new approach to consultancy. However, because the field has expanded considerably in the last few years, borrowing and co-opting ideas from fields such as linguistics and philosophy, systems thinking has become a large umbrella under which many ideas have come to reside. This chapter aims to distinguish those ideas which are central to our understanding and application of systems theory, and to define the concepts clearly enough so that the reader will feel well-armed with the conceptual tools necessary to proceed through the rest of the book.

The founder of General Systems Theory, von Bertalanffy (1956), was a biologist who found that traditional mechanistic models did not explain the behaviour of complex living organisms. He eventually made a distinction between physical laws and closed systems that do not interact with their environment, and dynamically interacting processes that affect living growing organisms. He was the first to emphasize that systems were "sets of elements standing in interrelation". Katz and Kahn (1966) defined systems theory as being "basically concerned with problems of relationships, of structure, and of interdependence, rather than with the constant attributes of objects". Systems theory has come to be known as the study of "wholeness" and "inter-dependence".

The world has moved on from General Systems Theory. The broader term, "systemic thinking", now incorporates some of the original concepts as well as new ideas developed since the 1960s. We have chosen to describe those concepts of systemic thinking which have proven to be helpful tools in our work as consultants, and not to present a comprehensive review of General Systems Theory or systems thinking. For a general discussion, readers should refer to Beishon and Peters (1972), Emery (1969), von Bertalanffy (1956), and Ashby (1958a, 1958b).

Systemic thinking is not an explanatory theory. It does not explain why organizations behave as they do. Rather, it is a framework for observing and understanding the world in terms of the connections amongst its many parts. It breaks the world into smaller units such as organizations, families, or communities and conceptualizes them as systems consisting of inter-connected parts. It is, of course, the type of thinking that many people apply to organizational problems—this is not new; but from the emergence of General Systems Theory in the 1950s to the present day, a growing number of thinkers and practitioners have teased-out the elements of this approach, analysed them in action, and applied them to many different fields. We now have a recognized body of knowledge known loosely as systemic thinking, and it is being applied increasingly to the worlds of organization and business. Because systemic thinking is a loose body of ideas and techniques, each practitioner will give his or her own version of which concepts are most important in using this approach. We have developed our own ideas from years of teaching and consulting within this model.

CREATING "PUNCTUATION"

If you read the letters "a t t e n d a n c e" as one word, it becomes "attendance". However, by introducing a capital letter and some punctuation, one can create an entirely new meaning from the same letters: "At ten, dance!"

The same letters but grouped and punctuated differently produce a new "system" of words.

A similar case can be applied to systemic thinking. One can argue that the universe is the *only* system (provided that there is an Observer to see it as a unified whole, but that's another story . . .), and anything less than the universe which we choose to call a system—such as a family, a town, an organization—is merely the product of the observer breaking up the world into his or her chosen parts. A furniture salesman and a molecular physicist may have completely different descriptions of the object we call "chair".

We, as observers, are continually "punctuating" or making distinctions about the world in which we live. We choose to see certain groupings as an organization because it is helpful for us to do so.

FROM CAUSE AND EFFECT TO SYSTEMIC THINKING

When we are strongly and directly affected by events going on around us, we tend to narrow our perspective and view these events in relation to ourselves, in relation to what has immediately triggered our response. We look for the people or objects or events "responsible" for triggering our response. It seems like a survival mechanism to find something to identify as a "cause" which we can then fight against in our own defence.

Take, for example, the difference we feel between a vague, worrying physical symptom and a diagnosis that defines the cause of the pain and prescribes a course of action. The process of finding and identifying causes offers a meaning for what is happening and a course of action to change the situation; and in many situations such simple cause-and-effect thinking is sufficient to change things and it is a comfort. For example, in an organization, the effect of poor communication may be "caused" by poor circulation of information, and the solution might simply be to distribute minutes of meetings to all the staff. However, our personal view of "what causes what" rarely reflects the reality of a complex organization. For an organization consisting of 10 or 100 or 1,000 employees, there will be individual reasons, departmental policies, and company cultures that affect the process of communication and make the meaning and understanding that much more complex.

The more narrow, cause-and-effect thinking is often referred to as **linear** (see Glossary) when it suggests a uni-directional relationship between the cause and the effect: "If I don't submit my report in time, the boss will be angry." This is often contrasted with the wider, more divergent systemic thinking which looks at the interaction of many causes and effects connected to the submission of the report. In fact, neither linear nor systemic thinking is better or more accurate in reflecting the nature of things. They are simply two perspectives on the same process. We use systemic thinking in our work because individuals tend to think in linear ways and the systemic perspective makes a difference to the way people see problems in organizations. Conversely, if people saw problems from a systemic perspective, it would be more helpful to introduce linear thinking to make a significant difference: "It sounds as though you didn't leave enough time to finish the report."

Systemic thinking is a discipline that offers a framework to observe and understand the complex, multi-layered processes within an organization. One of the postulates that create the framework of systemic thinking is:

- *The problem is not a problem in itself, but is a part of a larger process involving many "other" people, other "behaviours", and "other" meanings.*

So an application of systemic thinking to the communication problem above might lead one to understand that individuals feel they don't have the authority to suggest changes in what is communicated. The department may be so preoccupied with other issues that the managers have not realized the need to change a policy, and the culture of the organization may have survived up to now on a "need-to-know" basis rather than on a need to generate wider exchange of views.

As the reader, you may well be asking at this point, "So, what's new about this type of thinking? This is simply good organizational common sense."

Well, there is one crucial difference between good organizational common sense and what will be described as systemic thinking; and that difference lies in the way the observer of the problem is considered as *part* of the process that generates problems. In fact, the observer's view that a problem exists affects what he does, and this in turn affects what he observes and chooses to call a problem.

Since no one within an organization can be removed from the feedback loops that connect all the parts of the organization, the process of one person "observing" a problem in another person creates a false dichotomy between the observer and those observed, or between what is called the "observing system" and the "observed system" (Von Foerster, 1984). The systemic perspective encourages the observer to see himself as "part of the system" and to look for the effect that the act of observing and defining problems will have on what he is observing.

Several writers have taken this idea further by coining the term "problem-determined system" (Anderson, Goolishian, & Winderman, 1986). They described the way a group of people cluster around a specific problem, but since each is trying to solve it in relation to his own vested interest, problems remain unsolved.

FEEDBACK

The interdependence of the parts of a system is demonstrated through the feedback process. One part of a system (A) initiates some activity which has an effect on another part of the system (B). As a result, B alters its activity in relation to A, and this is perceived by A as feedback about the original activity. For example, if a department head sends a memo to a group of project team leaders asking for comments about a new policy, he is initiating an action, the response (or lack of response) to which will be perceived as feedback. The head (A) has initiated the first section of a feedback loop that goes out to the team leaders (B) and comes back to A, completing the loop (see Figure 1).

There are different types of feedback. Some of the team leaders may say this is a good policy—*positive feedback*—which sends the

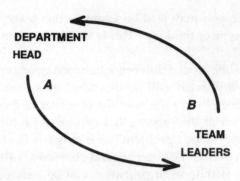

DEPARTMENT
HEAD

A

B

TEAM
LEADERS

Figure 1.   **Feedback loops**

message to continue in this direction or do more of the same. Other team leaders may comment that this is a bad policy—*negative feedback*—which communicates that the present condition should not continue and changes should be made. Both types of feedback are valuable; however, negative feedback can be more helpful in times of complexity and change, since it suggests possible directions in which an organization could shift in order to be more responsive to its environment.

We also find it helpful to use the concepts of "loose" feedback and "tight" feedback. For example, in some organizations there is a quick, direct, and relevant response to action in another part of the system. The feedback loop is tight because the response matches the original action without a lot of intervening events which may not be directly relevant. On the other hand loose feedback is that which is not seen to be immediately or directly responsive to an action. Most organizations that are not functioning well exhibit examples of loose feedback, particularly around the problem they face.

Staying with the example, one team leader may stay up all night to produce a five-page reply to her boss's request, while another is so busy he forgets to reply at all. These actions tell the boss something more than opinions about the new policy. In other words, there is feedback and there is *feedback*. The simple concept of feedback is not sufficient for understanding the complex processes going on in human systems. In order to account for some of this complexity, other concepts are necessary.

CONTEXT

The evolution of systems thinking has moved from the simple, mechanistic concept of a closed system to a dynamic, growing, open system that is "goal-directed" and "meaning-driven". Complex human systems exist for a purpose, and the purpose creates a context that in turn gives meaning to all of the activity that takes place in that context. Therefore feedback can only be received, or observed, by someone who is looking for feedback, and, depending on what context the observer is in, the same action can be interpreted to mean different things to different people.

In complex human systems like organizations, there are many overlapping contexts. For example, the aforementioned boss will be sending out the memo in one context of "wanting to receive comments about policy" but is also working in contexts of "I must continuously assess the work of my subordinates" and "I must respect the directives from my superiors". Each context provides the opportunity for someone to ascribe a context-specific meaning to those activities being observed from within the context.

These contexts can also be arranged hierarchically, in that the context about "doing the right thing in the eyes of the boss" exerts a strong influence on the contexts that are lower in the hierarchy, such as, "I must assess the work of my subordinates". The hierarchy of contexts has been described by two American communication theorists, Vernon Cronen and Barnett Pearce (1985), who made the point that while some contexts are larger and more inclusive—therefore higher in the hierarchy—all the contexts in the hierarchy exert mutual influences on each other, which means that the way the department head deals with his subordinates will influence the way he does the "right thing" for his boss.

Therefore, much of the focus of systemic thinking is trying to understand the contexts people are in and the meanings attributed to various activities. This enables us to locate the problems where they really belong, and when the picture of different contexts becomes clear, solutions are easier to find. Our experience has proven to us that many failed solutions result from an insufficient understanding of the myriad contexts that shape and maintain a problem. In practice, we spend considerable time making hypotheses about these various contexts and asking questions of people in different positions and different roles to understand the context they are operating from.

MEANING

A central assumption of systemic thinking is that human systems operate on the basis of the meaning that members ascribe to the activities around them. Clearly, if employees are in a context of anxiety about their jobs, they ascribe a particular meaning to a problem at work. The meaning may be: "There's a chance for me to advance my position at the expense of my colleague." But in a context in which employees feel secure and loyal to the organization, the same problem can mean: "This is an opportunity to work with my colleague to ensure the company gets the best deal."

Therefore, understanding an organization as a system is about understanding the many contexts and meanings people use to govern their behaviour. Typically a consultant using the systemic approach asks about the different ways people might understand an event, which respects the fact they live in different contexts, but also about how they order their different understandings the way they do. In other words, the consultant is trying to clarify the "meaning of the various meanings" or the meta-context (see Glossary) which determines why people see and understand what they do. Through this process the consultant is able to reach back to levels of meaning that the client may be unaware of but is influenced by nonetheless. Finally, this comes down to a method to help a client see more of the trees in the wood!

This process is illustrated in Figure 2. The employee in this case has become an observer of events going on around him in an organization. He is simultaneously in three different contexts (although the number can be limitless): Context A, which is arbitrarily placed at the top of the hierarchy, is characterized by his value statement: "I must support the strategic objectives of the company." Contexts B and C are "I must meet the technical needs of this assignment" and "I must maintain good relationships with my supervisors and colleagues", respectively. His perception—that is, what he sees and doesn't see, and how he understands what he sees—will be determined by the way these three contexts fit to-

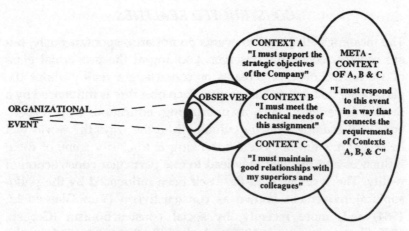

Figure 2. **Contexts and meta-context**

gether into a new "meta"-context. The process by which this meta-context is created will illuminate the underlying values that determine the way meanings are constructed. If the consultant can understand this process, he is half-way towards knowing where to direct further interventions. For example, if a client can articulate that he is only giving lip service to the context of "supporting strategic objectives" but that the predominant meaning he gives to problems is in fact determined by the need to "maintain good relationships", the consultant is more likely to focus on the most important issues.

Exercise A: To enable people to record different levels of meaning more easily, we frequently ask two people to get together to have a conversation about an everyday topic such as travel or food, but the participants are asked to try to convince the other person about a particular point of view without actually making it explicit. Then we bring in a third person to observe and listen to this conversation, but the observer is instructed to pay particular attention to the way these two are communicating rather than the content of what they are saying, and to arrive at some idea about the meaning of the whole act of communication. After five minutes the conversation stops and all three people discuss together what they thought was going on.

CONSTRUCTED REALITIES

The meanings attributed to events do not arise spontaneously, but are constructed by the observer. Looking at the proverbial glass of water, the observer creates or constructs a reality about the glass being half-full or half-empty. Each observer is influenced by a myriad experiences such as upbringing, education, work experience, and training, which gradually limit the ways the world will be seen. One aim of systemic thinking is to clarify some of these influences and the way they lead to one particular construction of reality. The systemic field has itself been influenced by the philosophical movement known as constructivism (Von Glasersfeld, 1984) and, more recently, by social constructionism (Gergen, 1985; Shotter & Gergen, 1989), which shifts the emphasis from the individual to the "individual in social interaction". Social constructionism proposes that realities are created by people communicating with each other through language, each influencing and limiting the range of responses from the other. In this approach, the area of interest is less the individual and more the network of interactions between people. This approach lends itself well to analysing the way realities are created in organizations.

We have chosen to call our approach to change management and consultation "constructionist" because it is a more focused concept than the broader term "systemic". Constructionist refers to our attention to the process by which people construct a view of organizational problems, and the process by which we attempt to join with our clients to construct together, or co-construct, a new story which includes the solution to the problem (see Glossary, **co-construction**).

LANGUAGE

Many practitioners within the field of systemic thinking believe that realities are constructed between people, and the process by which this happens is what we know as language. Language does not unlock the reality, but, rather, the reality is created through the process of two or more people engaged in "making language". As a result, analysing patterns in conversations or even memos between people becomes an important source of understanding how realities are created. A new field of study called discourse analysis has emerged to examine the process (Potter & Wetherell, 1987).

TEAM THINKING

If a system is a collection of many realities, a "multiverse" rather than a universe (Maturana & Varela, 1980), then the reality of an organization must in some way be created through the language and interaction of many people. For this reason, consultants using systemic thinking place great emphasis on team discussions of all types. It is through group discussions on specific topics that systemic thinking emerges in organizations. If a group of people are able to listen carefully and allow themselves to be influenced by others, while still contributing their views, new realities—belonging to no one person, but produced by the group process—emerge to define parts of the organization. This is called creating a "team mind" and is documented in another volume by one of the authors (Campbell, Draper, & Huffington, 1991a).

A variation on team discussions is the reflecting team (Andersen, 1990), in which one team sits apart and listens to another group discussing a problem. Following this, the first group "reflects" on what they have heard by presenting their own views for the second group to consider for their next discussion. We have found that one of the most effective and popular ways for people to experience how the team mind works to create systemic ideas is to take part in the "sequential discussion" exercise, and then discuss together what was learned during the exercise.

Exercise B: The "sequential discussion" exercise begins with four people sitting in a circle to discuss some case presentation or an article they have all read. They are asked to stick strictly to several ground rules to make the exercise work. (1) They must only speak in a sequential order, going around the circle following the person who precedes them. (2) When their turn arrives each person must first make a comment about the comment the previous person made—e.g. did they see it the same way or differently? (3) Following this, the person speaking adds a new idea or observation of his own, and passes the turn to the next person. (4) The participants are told to keep their comments brief, not to make speeches to convince others, but to drop their ideas into the middle of the circle and let others respond. After going around the circle three or four times the group stops to discuss the experience.

THE OBSERVER SITUATION

Systemic thinking is a means by which people can step back and observe their own position in the system. By this we mean clients become aware of the various influences upon them and the ways they influence others in the system—or, in this case, the organization. Typically, each of us sees the organization around us from our own perspective, as though it exists "out there", separate from our own influence upon it. So, for example, it is easier to see a communication problem in terms of other people not responding to memos or speaking openly at meetings, but it is difficult to see what we ourselves do that contributes to that process.

We aim to move people to the "observer's position" so that they can see their own contribution to problems in the organization. Once in this position, they can make changes that create new feedback loops and reverberate through other parts of the organization. When systemic thinking enables people to see themselves connected to various feedback loops, they are able to monitor complex feedback processes and make interventions that get beneath the surface to the daily transactions between people that shape the way the organization operates.

MEANING LEADS TO ACTION WHICH LEADS TO FURTHER MEANING

Understanding contexts and meaning is never enough. Any organization is shaped ultimately not by what people *think* but by what they *do*. The final goal of understanding the meanings people attribute to what they see is to understand their options for taking certain actions. In any social system, such as an organization, people learn about what is going on and how they should respond by observing various activities. It is not enough for managers to say that they believe in participative management: the employees must see the managers listening and soliciting suggestions—in action.

As consultants using systemic thinking, we have found it enorm-
ously helpful to explore the range of options for action which
follow from the meanings employees construe. Each action can be
discussed for its possible consequences—its gain or loss for the
different parts of the organization. Any action that is chosen and
then performed becomes feedback to other people and will contribute to the next stage of the evolving meanings that people create
about the organization. Figure 3 illustrates the way any action
(Action 1) acquires meaning (Meaning 1) when observed in a context. This leads to new actions which are observed in a new
context, and so on.

> *Exercise C:*   In order to enable people to experience the move-
> ment from action to meaning and back again, we ask them to
> speak together in pairs. One of them acts as interviewer and asks
> the other to think of one small thing that they might do—i.e. one
> way they might behave differently—to create some change in
> their organization. Then they are asked to think about the mean-
> ing of this action—e.g. by describing the possible effects this
> might have on the beliefs, relationships, or procedures in the
> organization. The partner is then asked to think about a second
> action they might carry out as a result of seeing the changes
> from the first action. This is followed by a discussion of the
> meaning or the effect that the second act would have on the
> organization, and so on. After about ten minutes, the roles can
> be swapped and the exercise is completed with a discussion
> between the two about what was learned from the exercise.

CHANGE

The original General Systems Theory conceived of a mechanistic,
closed system based on the principle of homeostasis: input must
equal output. The *open* system of the organization interacting with
both its internal and external environments is more complex. The
feedback to any activity becomes multi-layered and can therefore
have consequences in many parts of an organization. This means
that change is not a uni-directional process. It involves a shifting of
many different contexts within an organization. This may happen
in many ways: for example, the Government may change the larger

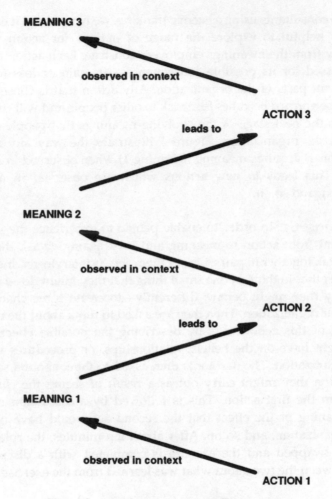

Figure 3. **Action, context, and meaning**

commercial context through new legislation; a competitor may change the context by introducing a new product to the market; or employees may demand a change in working conditions or salary, which leads to a re-ordering of commercial priorities.

In systemic thinking, a distinction that has been found particularly fruitful is between "first-order" and "second-order" change. First-order change involves the alteration in the activity of parts of a system that enables it to adapt or correct its equilibrium in response to external changes of a non–system-threatening degree, without fundamentally changing the rules governing the inter-relationship of the parts of the system. An example would be the action of a production manager in reducing production rates when faced with rising stock levels following an unexpected decline in despatches/sales. This type of change is appropriate where no fundamental alteration in the external environment occurs—for example, where the manager "knows" that demand will eventually recover.

Second-order change, by comparison, occurs where the altera-tion in the activity of parts of a system reflects the evolution of new "rules" governing their inter-relationship. This occurs usually in response to some radical change in the external environment. Second-order change is therefore often dis-continuous with the past, sudden and unpredictable in its full ramifications. An ex-ample would be where, as a result of a radical shift in competitive cost structures, internal "producing" units are placed at "arm's length" to "purchasing" units and in competition with external sources of supply to those purchasing units.

Although organizations, like the environment in which they live, are changing all the time, decisions must be made to lead the changes in one direction rather than another. The systemic approach maintains that organizations can be led and influenced, but they cannot be pushed. The analogy of the sailboat is more appropriate than the car. The driver of a car is in control of the speed and direction of the vehicle, whereas a sailor must steer in accordance with the wind and waves and has a more complemen-tary relationship with the environment.

Nevertheless, the process of change must be managed, and this is done by discussing the effects that change in one part of the system will have on other parts in the context of the overall organization. This type of discussion creates the higher context of organizational change, or the "change of many changes".

Our experience has proven to us that in order for change to work its way through a whole organization, each component, whether it be individuals in smaller organizations or departments in larger ones, must be considered for its influence on others in the change process and the effect of the process on that component. In setting up such discussions, we find many organizations are stuck because they cannot envisage the consequences of various changes they might make. In these situations it is very helpful to pose hypothetical questions about future consequences and to study the gains and losses to parts of the organization of the different options. Systemic practitioners and consultants have been using "hypothetical" or "future" questions as a central technique in their work for many years (Campbell et al., 1991a; Penn & Sheinberg, 1986).

> *Exercise D*: A simple exercise to illustrate the power of discussing the hypothetical future is to ask pairs to interview each other about where they or their organization might be in one, two, or three years. When they have a picture in their mind, one can discuss the possible routes for moving in that direction and the gains and losses along the way of those particular changes.

THE FIT AMONGST PARTS OF THE SYSTEM

Although systemic thinking can be applied to the relationship between teams or departments in an organization, the emphasis in this volume will be on the individual as the basic unit that makes up the larger system. The *"individual in context"* is the observer who perceives feedback from others, decides on the meaning of the feedback, and chooses an appropriate action.

People in organizations are ultimately trying to balance their individual needs for respect, power, wealth, achievement, and belonging with the group needs of cooperation, following orders, carrying out difficult tasks, personal sacrifices, etc. When the personal gains can be met through work, an employee will be satisfied and should continue to work for the good of the company; however, if work is unsatisfying or threatening to an individual's well-being, he will begin to work more for himself than for the company. In this scenario, an employee tries to build his own personal security or power base, which usually conflicts with the needs of the organization.

A system is a "whole greater than the sum of its parts" and what makes it greater is the process by which the component parts work together. If they work in harmony—if they fit—the whole is seen to be integrated and efficient. Therefore the systemic thinker is always interested in "problems of fit" between (a) the component parts and (b) the components and the whole. The components should be in a relationship such that they contribute to the smooth working of the whole—the organization.

While the components of a system must "fit", there must also be sufficient difference and diversity among the parts for each to be demarcated and defined in relation to the other. When an organization reaches a certain size (some would say 8 to 10 employees), it can no longer carry out its business efficiently without delegation and differentiation of tasks. In this new context, the organization must clearly demarcate itself into different parts if it is to define its tasks and utilize resources effectively. This diversity makes the organization more flexible and responsive to new demands from the outside world, able to move constantly to balance itself and adjust to new feedback from internal and external sources. The organization may experience this constant movement as a tension between structure and consistency on the one hand, and diversity and new ideas on the other.

Once the organization has responded to the need for differentiation, certain people inevitably have more access to information or resources than others, and it can be said that these people have more "power" and are higher in the hierarchy. Leaders are required to dream and suggest new directions, while managers are necessary to control operations and see that the parts fit together. From the systemic viewpoint, it is not helpful to see this "power" as an attribute of a role or a particular person. It is more usefully seen as an *outcome* of people agreeing to relate in certain ways (or seeing only a particular way of relating as open to them). In other words, power is defined within the context in which it is exercised. Senior managers may have the formal "power" to plan and control the work of employees. Less obvious, but essential to the working relationship, however, is the workers' "power" to help keep the company in business by the way in which they are prepared to do their work, perhaps by asserting their valid contribution to the planning and control of their operations. In this view, it is they who have the "power" to keep senior management in employment (managers tend to see the hire-and-fire decision rather differently!).

The manner in which these different aspects of power are activated and balanced out suggests the shifts in interaction that may
lead to a more effective use of resources. As in dealing with the
tension between stability and change, so also with the concept of
power—the challenge for any organization is to maintain a dynamic balance.

FROM THEORY TO ACTION . . .

All of the ideas and concepts in this chapter have to be applied
with the aid of specific techniques in work with individuals,
groups, and organizations. The methodology and some of the techniques we have developed as constructionist consultants are
described in the book. However, several are worth mentioning at
the outset, not only because the terms will be used in case discussions, but also because they represent the essence of the systemic
stance that is so helpful to problem-bound client systems. They
concern hypothesizing, **neutrality,** and **circularity** (see Glossary).

As we begin to gather information from the client system,
we construct a number of what we call **working hypotheses** (see
Glossary), which we acknowledge will always form only a partial
picture, but which guide us to look for information in certain areas
to clarify how the organization is working. When we talk to individuals and small groups, we often use a technique we call
"systemic questioning" (also referred to as **circular questioning,**
see Glossary). At the same time as helping gather a different level
of information to test our hypotheses, this technique also has the
effect of engaging clients in thinking about their own position from
a systemic perspective. This questioning technique is directed at
the connections between parts of the organization, at the way
meanings lead to certain actions and actions support certain meanings. As we become aware of the inter-connections in the client's
meaning system, we are able to construct a **systemic hypothesis**
(see Glossary) which will help us decide how we can help the client
find new options for action that do not contain the problem. For
example, this helps us recognize when it is important for us to take
a particular position to test out an organization's response to an
idea. At other times, we may see the need to work from a position
of **neutrality** (see Glossary). In this case we would not take a posi-

tion, which might close down further exploration, but remain curious to explore further, with an equal, or neutral, interest in the full range of views on a subject.

In Chapter 2, we show how we have applied the theoretical concepts of the present chapter in practice in order to helpfully **reframe** (see Glossary) conventional ways of approaching typical management issues of leadership, communication, change, and control.

CHAPTER 2

Application of systemic concepts in organizational work

Shifting from expertise to co-creation

In the first chapter we explored a number of systemic and social constructionist concepts which over the past twenty years have provided a powerful stimulus to family and individual therapists practising in the United States and Europe. In this chapter we continue this journey—management consultants trying out systemic and social constructionist ideas in their usual domain of work with large-scale organizations. We explore a number of the dilemmas we experience as we ply our increasingly systemic trade, and outline some of the responses we have developed to both earn a living and stay "systemic enough" . It shows how we have tried to make changes in our thinking, making the bridge between theory and "praxis" (theory in action). A key feature of the learning we outline in this chapter is the challenge of finding ways of using the concept of feedback to provide links between "universal" approaches and "local" contexts of action.

The chapter subtitle indicates one way in which we understand our challenge: while we espouse the benefits of social constructionist thinking, most of our clients, at least initially, expect us to provide expert advice. This advice typically would be based on experience of solutions to apparently similar problems in other situations but, given a **positivist** (see Glossary) perspective, would be seen to have universal applicability (see Glossary, **universal solutions**). In the field of management, there is a long history of such positivist-orientated research aimed at "discovering" the "best way" to organize, provide leadership, deliver quality, and so on. It is this expectation—that "local" difficulties can best be solved through the application of "universal" good practice—that lies at the heart of the problems faced by many change and effectiveness improvement programmes. And it is this belief that we as budding systemic practitioners have had to confront and deal with in developing our practice.

In the course of making a living as a systemic consultancy, we have found that there are three main problems for which we have to find solutions:

- how to find ways of marketing our services to potential clients—"Well, what actually do you do?"

- how to do what is seen as useful work by the various multi-level stakeholders [all those who have a particular stake or interest in what happens in the organization, not just the shareholders] we meet in our assignments—"How are you actually helping *me* solve this problem?"

- how to stay connected long enough to help clients deal with the feedback and second-phase change difficulties—"*Now* I realize what it is you offer that is different!"

In seeking to resolve these, we have over the past few years identified ten overlapping but nevertheless particular dimensions of consulting approach which seem to make a difference. In doing this, and despite the problem of *incommensurability* (Bernstein, 1983), we feel we have been able to help our clients recognize the benefits of leaving aside some of their positivist expectations of expertise to embrace a more contextual and local view on what counts as valid knowledge and effective problem solving. We have grouped these ten *"reframes"* into three broad categories, which we find useful in thinking about the new stance needed by consultants who wish to practise in this way.

The first category we have identified is to do with the *observing position* that the consultant needs to take up in order to offer this service—what is called the **second-level cybernetics** position (see Glossary and Chapter 6). In this category there are two reframes.

Reframe 1—From universal to local solutions

Every year, organizations spend heavily to develop managers in line with new strategies based on a range of apparently universal "panaceas". But the outcomes are frequently depressing. Managers have described to us how "high-profile campaigns turn into jugger-nauts ... driven by forms and slogans". Research shows that two-thirds of quality programmes grind to a halt, failing to pro-duce expected returns. Other senior managers have expressed to us their frustration at the high decay rate of new skills training, so that within a year the intended new behaviours are still not yet in evidence, let alone the new cultures that were promised. Interpersonal skill matrices, problem-solving approaches, and various coaching styles are just not used, seemingly pushed out by the difficulty of immediate tasks.

We think managers find it difficult to hang on to training in new skills and use these to help them in their actual work because of the thinking that underlies conventional manager development pro-grammes. These overlook the *network of relations* and organization cultures in which managers operate and which determine whether new skills will get used. They also introduce these new ideas as though they had *universal relevance*, failing to make the connection with the "local" experience of the manager, which contributes to the existing **mind-map** (see Glossary) that is used to decide on behaviour in difficult situations. Finally, these programmes deliver the new ideas too often as *instructions* in a format that kills any possibility of dialogue from which personal ownership of change can emerge.

In a large public sector organization, we were asked to run a series of one-day workshops for 300 senior "purchasers" and their key internal "provider" managers to help initiate the launch of a new internal market operation. During the course of difficult morn-ing sessions (an experience that was repeated 15 times!), it was obvious that most of the participants shared a very negative view of the top-down changes that had been introduced. The dominant story was one of complete disempowerment and fatalism: "It's wholly wrong, but we can't do anything about it."

An important exercise introduced after the damning feedback of the opening session involved participants working in mixed groups to assess the current context and develop their *own* strategy for dealing with the problems the organization was facing. What was amazing was how often the different subgroups on each and every occasion came up with stories that seemed almost identical to the "vision" (or "what" changes) that had been handed down as tablets of stone. But there was a difference now—as they now obviously all *shared* a new vision of what had to be, there was in fact a lot that they could do to negotiate the "how" of the changes. And as their new story took shape, more and more people seemed able to discover examples of "exceptions" to the old "dominant story" (White, 1991). The confidence generated by these events led to a different quality of feedback to senior management, which improved the level of dialogue about strategy implementation.

In our view, ideas, policies, and programmes become meaningful and useful only when there are opportunities for interaction between those holding the "corporate intent" and those with the "local experience" who are responsible for their implementation.

Reframe 2—From observed to observing systems

Among the management "cookbooks" about the latest "big idea", you will find many that have in their titles something to do with "leadership". They all reflect another assumption of positivist thinking: that change is a process that must be stimulated by outside forces, because the natural state of affairs at best will do no more than maintain the status quo or, more likely, allow organizational/energy levels to dissipate to the lowest point. Change is envisaged as a linear process moving through stages, with each one depending on the preceding one for inputs and then feeding outputs to succeeding stages. This world view becomes visible in many managers when one questions them on the style of leadership associated with success, particularly that displayed by the chief executive, and on their beliefs about the attitudes and abilities of many of the people in their organizations:

- "Ordinary employees don't really know how to improve corporate performance, but top management do."

- "Staff, therefore, need to be told and taught how to be concerned about quality and customer service."

- "They are more likely to work better if they feel their job may at any moment be taken away from them and if most of their pay is dependent on their own work output."

- "In time people are likely to relax into old habits and become too secure, so good top managers keep things changing to keep the pressure on."

These attitudes are often masked and made more acceptable by the sincerity and personal commitment these managers show to the organization and the well-being of their workforce. But this does not alter their fundamental importance. For along with the thinking of "them" as separate from "us", of managers from workers, of purchasers from providers, of the company from suppliers, there goes the tendency to believe that the performance of the whole system can be *directed* from the outside. Reality is out there, and, if one is sufficiently determined, it can be operated on. The chief executive *can* decide on the cause of problems, close factories, change people, and virtually single-handedly start turning the business around. And then things will really change, and business results improve. But why is it that many such situations have a habit of reverting to old patterns once the all-powerful head has taken the pressure off . . . ?

Although the chief executive (and others) may believe he is able to act effectively in a linear way *on* the organization, we try to identify examples that show there is a *two-way* influencing process at work in which the organization is also producing reactions from the chief executive, and that he is just as much a part of the problem as any other. So while we listen and try to understand the message the chief executive believes he is telling his people, we are alert for feedback that might suggest his people have heard something different, and how that something different is having an effect on his own behaviour. We point out, whenever we can, the connections that appear to exist between their beliefs, important relationships between members of the problem-owning system, and the results that they are concerned about. And then when we join the chief executive and others in the process of defining problems and creating solutions, we try to help them become more aware of how through the operation of **reflexivity** (see Glossary), they are all *in* the system and *a part of* the meaning making process—not independent operators, observers, or victims of something happening "out there".

A clear example of this was provided by a very successful privately owned international financial services firm that asked for our help with a change initiative to do with improving customer service. The chairman was clear about the problem—the professionalism of people in the administration of deals once they had been concluded. He wanted an event to be facilitated where these ideas would be worked on and internalized by his people—high-powered and creative deal-makers with a strong element of entrepreneurship in their make-up. He also had a more covert objective: to create an opportunity for his direct reports to show their leadership qualities. This would allow him to plan his own withdrawal from daily management concerns and eventual retirement, without causing loss of performance. His belief was that he could achieve the changes he envisaged by the appropriate design of an event involving the whole organization, while he took up the role of a detached observer.

During our initial discussions with the senior management group, we began to form a hypothesis that connected the leader to his problem. There had been earlier change initiatives. At one time, the chairman's worry had been about growth and critical mass. The organization had responded by putting on headcount and winning new business. Then the worry changed to quality and profitability of business and controls. A divisional structure was created. The organization responded by internal competition to achieve the best "bottom line", and "parochial" barriers became the worry. This was the point at which the chairman introduced his current worry about efficiency and the theme of management professionalism. From the story thus far, we expected the beliefs of staff, formed by their context, to determine their next response.

We designed an event for the whole organization in which we could make it "safe enough" for these beliefs to be expressed. This would allow the chairman to hear the extent to which his actions in the past and his present intent were creating his problem, and how his own actions in response were sustaining it. To "prime" the event, we used examples of beliefs we had picked up as being typical and significant for the future. Two examples were: "new business is the life-blood of this company"; and "over-management creates bureaucracy and stifles creativity". Using the fishbowl format [an activity where one subgroup discusses a topic while the other listens; no interaction is permitted] for discussions, it soon became quite clear to everybody, including the chairman, that his own past actions seemed to have created a belief that only he could combine the role of business producer and business manager. The systems he had put in place, notably the commission system, also now stood in the way of change. Genuine change would be dependent on mutually agreed shifts in the idea of leadership and the relationships between founder and aspiring successors.

We were not surprised to hear, some time after the event, that the chairman's plans had undergone considerable modification. The quick-fix solutions had given way to a greater use of developmental routes to change. Unhooking the chairman from the problem system was now seen as a more complex process, requiring time.

In our view, adaptiveness and flexibility in complex organizational systems is enhanced when self-appointed change agents are able to connect their own previous and anticipated actions to the problems of change, of the "resistance" that they are seeking to manage and control. Change programmes start to deliver when such people are able to see themselves as an integral part of management processes that reflect their place within the problem system, rather than as independent manipulators of "things".

Once the consultant has developed the stance of operating from the second-level cybernetics position, the focus shifts: to helping clients inquire in a participative way in order to get at the underlying issues that separate people; and then to helping them use this as feedback on how

*others in the system are understanding the meaning of the action that is
being taken. This second category of consulting skills centres on* generating and using valid knowledge to steer the processes of change: *it
comprises four of the reframes we have identified.*

Reframe 3—From part to whole

Within the prevailing **paradigm** (see Glossary) of the world of
business, an important example of the positivist belief in "management as science" is the **reductionist** (see Glossary) methodology.
To find out about how things work or why there are problems in an
organization, this methodology advocates "stripping content of
contaminating (confounding) influences (variables) so that the inquiry can converge on truth and explain nature as it really is and
really works, leading to the capability to predict and control"
(Guba & Lincoln, 1989). Once this is done, short-term causal linkages become clearer, allowing events to be predicted or controlled.
Underlying this approach is the conception of "nature" as like a
great machine in which everything is linked in a pre-determined
and predictable way.

In management, this paradigm first became formalized in the
work of Frederick Taylor in turn-of-the-century America. He believed that the welfare of new immigrant workers could best be
served by studying their work in detail, identifying discrete parts,
rationalizing how each part could be done by experiment, and then
training the unskilled workers intensively so that they could perform these parts of the whole task with fluency. His paternalistic
vision was quickly dropped as owners of firms realized the potential of his methods for raising the earning power of their assets.
Since those days, not only has polarization in the perceived interests of workers and bosses become entrenched, but so also has the
widespread belief in the primacy of management by specialization.
Even the rise of systems thinking, although it offered a counter to
the reductionist view, could not supplant this essentially hierarchical, functionalist, and fragmenting view of management.

Our work as constructionist practitioners has been aided by the
changes among Western companies spurred by the need to counter
the success of Japanese methods and strategies. There has been a
reduction in levels of management, greater emphasis on teams, and

the empowerment of "front-line" staff to control their work. We are still a long way, however, from seeing the general acceptance of a "hermeneutic" methodology of management—the encouragement of a "continual dialectic of iteration, analysis and critique" among all those involved in a problem, leading to the emergence of a shared view (Guba & Lincoln, 1989). Perhaps we should not be surprised that aspects of this approach are found in the Japanese strategic policy-making ritual of *ringi*. This sees policy proposals being passed for discussion and review by a wide range of managers, each of whom is encouraged to identify areas of contention that need attention. In this way, all perceptions of constraints and values have a chance to inform the final policy. The process takes time, but adds the value of coherence and commitment to the final decision. In our practice, we have been able to persuade some clients of the benefits of moving towards this more "emergent" end of the continuum.

The experiential evidence of benefits from attempting such a shift have long been available in the work of social scientists such as Lewin, McGregor, and Lippitt in the United States, as well as in the pioneering discoveries in Yorkshire coalmines by Emery and Trist (1960). Following Weisbord (1990), the paradigm shift we propose to clients is:

Away from	*Towards*
"solve the problem"	"create the future"
"bring in the expert"	"help people learn"
"identify the accountable manager"	"involve everybody"
"find the right technique"	"find a helpful process"
"find the best way"	"find a better way"
"get a quick fix"	"improve continuously"

We were approached by the managing director of a building products manufacturing company, part of a major multinational. His concern was to find an alternative means of generating change in his operation. Until the present, he had identified and pushed through a range of measures that had stripped away fixed costs, rationalized product offerings, and delegated decisions closer to the "shop floor". His concern was that this style of changing was creating its own block to further change. He was aware his management team had become so thinly stretched that they had no capacity for thinking about, let alone managing, further changes. The workforce, deprived of their supervisory cushion in the last round of change, felt too vulnerable to act in line with their new devolved responsibilities. Yet the pressures in the competitive environment were intensifying and were likely to require greater flexibility in future, and more frequent changes of product formulations.

We focused on the implications for this operation of staying within the present paradigm of functional specialist-led change, both to show a shared concern with the position of our potential client, but also to amplify the sense of blockage he felt and to increase his willingness to entertain thinking about options from outside the paradigm.

We used Lippitt's "future inventing" approach (Lippitt, 1983) to give him the experience of a way of thinking about issues that was different from the depressingly familiar problem-resolving process. This future turned out to be about a workforce much more proactive in change, with a management team less involved in daily firefighting and so more able to develop peoples' skills as well as monitoring the company's strategic position, the better to galvanize pre-emptive planning for evolving threats.

To open up awareness of a way of operationalizing his invented future, we shared with the managing director our systemic analysis of the change process. We joined in "sweating" over the dilemma of how to get people acting in line with that new relationship between management and staff when the vision for that relationship was held only by the managing director. How could people buy-in to radical change unless they could see how that change would work out in everyday relations; and yet how could they believe in this possibility when management, in proposing radical change, seemed to be reinforcing its usual hierarchical prerogatives?

The resolution of the dilemma involved using this desired form of relating between management and staff as the vehicle for evolving the proposals for a different and radical response to the competitive threats facing the organization. We proposed a series of "whole organization" workshops, bringing managers and staff together as people sharing a joint concern and interest in their organization. Our client began to see how letting people in on "inventing their future" like this would create the experiences from which could come a willingness to believe that different options for managing the plant could work. They might be reassured that these options were preferable to the present situation where stressed specialist experts pressured disempowered and insecure operatives to adopt new procedures.

In our view, the inclusion of wider representation of the system in the processes of policy formulation will produce different and more radical change proposals, speed up their acceptance, and lead to a greater commitment level from system members.

Reframe 4—From debate to dialogue

Although we are often not aware of it, *metaphor* exercises a pervasive influence in everyday life—not just in language, but in thought and action. An example offered by Lackoff and Johnson (1980) is the metaphor "argument is war". In everyday working when we use common expressions such as "His case was shot down in flames" and "How are we going to attack his position?", we are not just *talking* about arguments as war, we are actually engaging in a win-or-lose struggle. The way management and trades unions negotiate, and the debates between different political parties as they go about legislating, make the point clear: "argument is war" is a metaphor that many live by in our culture.

These tendencies modelled in our language are reinforced by other features of the organizations people work in:

* *Structure:* Many organization structures are strongly characterized by hierarchy, power, and control. Despite the increasing acceptance of the importance of showing a greater customer orientation, each layer in the structure often seems to exist to service the functioning of higher levels. It also seems to be accepted that role functions, behaviours, and norms of performance are laid down by higher authority without recourse to appeal. While, on the surface, business may be carried out

politely, many staff feel powerless to confront openly what they may see as ineffective or unfair arrangements. In order to survive or prosper, many instead strive to ensure that they meet the standards that seem demanded of them, often in a self-policing way (see Sheridan, 1980). As problems are believed to arise principally from insufficient "socialization" of staff, these standards are clarified and reinforced by a whole raft of policies and programmes that dominate the thinking and practice of management today—to do with *the right way* to think about selection, performance management, training, communication, and rewards.

- *Problem solving:* Many organization structures tend to enshrine a fragmented and piecemeal approach where problems are passed to the appropriate specialists for diagnosis and solution. Often these solutions are based on what is seen as "best practice" from that function's particular point of view and from experience gained from apparently similar situations encountered before in other different organizations. Even where such functional specialists are encouraged to take more account of the system as a whole, as in the latest fashion for process re-engineering, it is usually only a partial aspect of the system that is subject to diagnosis. The *dynamic interaction* between the technical, social, and commercial aspects of an issue is seldom considered, nor are the needs and values of the human component of the wider system. Challenges to this narrow approach to problem resolution face an uphill battle as functional expertise confronts everyday concerns and inhibitions.

- *Change:* This is linked to another belief of managers to do with change and communication. Many believe strongly in the possibility of **instructive interaction** (see Glossary)—in which communication is assumed to be a one-way process: people can be told what they need to do and how to do it, and effective changes in behaviour will follow. Such managers suffer from the widely shared delusion that words have a single meaning (i.e. *my meaning*) and that those receiving the message have identical goals and criteria and share the same understanding of context. When the required changes in behaviour are not forthcoming, or are poorly executed, the assumption is that the message needs to be repeated or reinforced—"people are either not intelligent enough or they are being resistant". In such climates, differences in view are not seen as potentially valid or even useful, and so the stratagems and armaments of debate and negotiation are seen as more relevant. Change is seen as about getting people to *do* things differently. The belief is that these changes can be introduced most efficiently by simply *instructing* the hierarchy; if this doesn't work, then other mechanisms of persuasion need to be employed.

In sympathy with the "argument is war" metaphor, these polarizing perspectives reinforce the perception that "difference" is threatening, and that it would be just too risky to engage in more open-ended processes. Such assumptions energize a common behaviour we notice among managers—the battle to *"be right"* and to voice the *"one best way"* of dealing with issues. While this bias towards confrontation, holding one's position, and winning might seem to be the only sensible stance in today's competitive world, such behaviour can often lead to a sense of stuckness and isolation for the protagonists themselves and others around them, and repress the creative instincts that could open up other possibilities.

This problem was well illustrated during a long-drawn-out merger process between two public development agencies. A small working group detailed the mechanics of the merger, while a larger group of thirty senior executives met to air issues they believed were raised by the merger plans. A big problem was that the statutory constraints on the merger process meant that there was an inevitable mismatch: executives' expectations that *leadership* would be able to address their anxieties about the impact of the merger on work and relationships did not mesh with leadership's ability to reveal anything of substance which matched those expectations. This clash of expectations was experienced as a "loss of trust" between the working group and the executive group. It was expressed as a concern about the quality of communication. Yet the two groups had met fortnightly for the best part of a year! However, as we attended some of their meetings, we realized that in this culture it was more important for each of these managers to "debate the truth" in an adversarial manner, to be seen to be holding the high ground of "true seeing", than it was for them collectively to find common ground about possibilities for action.

Plainly a different sort of meeting was needed that would give them a new experience as a group, from which they would be able to see their situation differently enough to feel that "communication" had been achieved. The intervention we chose was a workshop for the whole group around the theme of *stability and change*. Our hypothesis was that positioning the idea of change as a "normal" process—with natural coping mechanisms, for example, being able to hold onto important values while letting other things go to embrace something new—would help reduce the sense of disconnection these executives felt about the future. In this way, "communication" would then become less of a pressing problem, and managers would find it possible to actually take some action.

Often in these situations it is very easy for people to fall into an "all or nothing" stance. By surfacing current dilemmas and exploring different views of the gains and losses associated with each, we hoped to give them opportunities to "rediscover" options for action which they had lost sight of. In other words, we hoped that they would be able to construct a much more discriminating view of what was and was not possible. For example, we asked them to think about what they might feel able to do if they could challenge their own distinction between the proper role of "leader" and "manager" in times of change. We had a hunch that this "playing" with different roles and positions on issues would create an experience that in total would help them realize how much information was already available to help them relate differently to action possibilities within their system. It would thus help them appreciate the many ways in which *they* could identify and construct valid information to meet their need for more "communication".

We were not disappointed by what happened in following these ideas. Despite the continuing climate of uncertainty, most managers were able to see a wider range of possible actions that they could now take, and the presenting concern about the lack of communication about the merger took on a less prominent position in their thinking. This experience of the power of "inquiry", the seeking of understanding rather than debates about "the truth", had a powerful impact on these managers—one that was frequently re-called over the succeeding two years as they dealt with the merger and initial shakedown of the new organization.

In our view the adoption of a more relativist position, expressed through dialogical inquiry (rather than the debating processes encouraged by positivist beliefs), can bring forth a greater degree of awareness of other options for change, other explanations that dis-solve problems or that can lead to new ideas for change.

Reframe 5—From detail to dynamic complexity

We are frequently asked by clients to help in the "management of change". When we delve into the background to this request, we often find that we are being asked to help in the latest attempt to introduce "a change that will actually make a change". The client organization may in fact be "change groggy", lying low waiting for the next corporate initiative derived from the latest management best-seller. This situation reflects an impasse into which a positivist management paradigm condemns change agents and inspirational leaders to labour fruitlessly.

Many of these change programmes are built around an idea of "what" it is that needs to be done differently. One method that has became increasingly popular with consultants and top managers alike is the so-called "training cascade". In this process, the organization develops or buys a highly structured and packaged training programme and then drives it down successively through the levels the organization, in line with a tight timetable. The idea is that each level will be indoctrinated just before their direct reports, so that they can then manage the implementation of the new thinking.

From critical reports and our experience of the effectiveness of many total quality programmes, this process seldom leads to the smooth transition from espousal to enactment as the cascade spills down the hierarchy. There is usually little opportunity for review of the feedback arising at each level or potentially difficult but useful inquiries into whether and why there might be resistance. The pressure is almost entirely on keeping the high-visibility first phase of change effort going. The problem with this whole approach to change is that it does not deal with the *dynamics* of the situation, both within the organization and in the environment in which it operates. Changing is envisaged as something that can be instructed, planned, and controlled. The challenge is seen as one of needing to be sufficiently detailed and comprehensive in handling the complexity of change.

An example may help to show how we apply our constructionist "lenses" when we are asked to help cascade a programme of change down an organization. A major pharmaceutical company was intent on introducing a set of new corporate values which were to be translated into daily behaviour change throughout the organization. They had prepared a cascade plan built around a group of in-house trainers who would involve line management in training sessions to enable them in turn to train their subordinates in new skills. We explored the context of this plan, the relationship pattern that had emerged around the question of its implementation, and the dynamic complexities anticipated from implementing the plan. Our main focus throughout was on the underlying dilemmas facing our client manager, who was in ultimate charge of the success of this change effort.

The shape of the thinking that emerged reflected a number of important systemic/constructionist principles. The leadership change required was a shift of thinking away from a concern with the specification of detail and the solution of problems. Instead, there needed to be an awareness of the dilemmas always involved in addressing the interests of multiple stakeholders, and in the dynamic complexity of change itself. The metaphor emerged of the corporate helmsman (Hampden-Turner, 1990), not holding to a fixed course but constantly redefining the course between conflicting priorities; not solving problems but constantly *re-solving* them on the basis of feedback.

This implied a change in the nature of the proposed cascade process, too. From a didactic, one-way push process, the idea emerged of building in conversations *across* levels and functions. The cascade became not a vehicle of a single change—first-order change at that—but rather a process for achieving an on-going conversation within the organization about the ways of becoming better at fulfilling the vision set out by leadership. Second-order change would be achieved by moving participants from the level of knowing something different, to practising, living, and hence enabling others to know and practise. By building feedback in as part of the process, the essential reflexive element would be facilitated—so that people would know how they knew, know how they practised, and know how they enabled. We called this aspect of the cascade introducing the "how of the how" into change programmes.

In our view, change "leadership" becomes more effective when it switches from a focus on the detailing of processes in support of the intended changes to the management of meaning of the feedback from the ongoing dynamic complexity of the change process itself.

Reframe 6—From quantification to appreciation

Look at many fashionable distinctions in management "theory" from a different perspective and you may see the pattern of thinking that represents such a challenge to a systemic constructionist consultant. There is clearly a belief in reality as something that is stable, independent of context and observer, and measurable. Indeed, there is a privileging of measuring as a management activity. Its necessity in financial control and its utility in process control has encouraged its spread into the marketing and personnel functions. In the latter area, you now have performance, competence, attitudes, and behaviours measured and their future course or effects predicted by reference to norm groups or correlations. The role of context in these measures and the effect of the measuring process itself on what is being measured are either unremarked or ignored.

Even revered gurus find it difficult to stem the flood of measuring. For example, W. Edwards Deming (1982) regularly demonstrated the danger of individual performance measurement in isolation from consideration of the influence of the system; yet even he could do little to deflect and shelter workers from the demotivating impact of individual performance rewards. This particular view of motivation and accountability increasingly dominates corporate thinking, particularly in the public sector, but it only seems to frustrate the intent of top management: what they are doing to introduce a new level of "performance management" often has the opposite effect.

In one creative public sector organization, we have seen massive changes in structure, processes, and culture being reinforced by a huge, centrally driven "performance review" effort. It seems characterized by an unswerving belief in "unshakeable facts", more typical of the private sector (Geneen, 1985). The very diverse set of operating units are being required to complete lengthy and standard *written* dossiers on current capability and operating performance. These are submitted to scrutiny in arm's-length "star chamber" meetings, with comparison of quantitative performance indicators made across the different areas of output, leading inevitably to some form of re-targeting exercise. While learning and benefits can arise from such an exercise, the implied focus on only that which can be quantified, in an activity where matters of personal taste dominate, has its dangers. The "context-stripping" nature of the centrally focused procedure and the lack of opportunities for the "tops" and "bottoms" to engage in a more flexible *dialogue* puts at risk precisely what needs to be appreciated: the unique characteristics of local context, vision, genre, working method, and motivation that have led to these units being leaders in their fields.

This seems an excellent example of the more "appreciative" position stated by Guba and Lincoln (1989) that "if something can be measured, the measurement may fit into some construction, but it is likely at best to play a *supportive* role" (our italics). In a few parts of this organization, enlightened managers are starting to hold development seminars. Here opportunities are being created for the "tops" and the "bottoms" to engage in a more flexible dialogue in which mutual respect and understanding encourages a realistic search for the "new information" that leads to the development of new performance levels.

Another client situation has brought us into contact with the compulsory competitive tendering (CCT) procedures that local authorities have been required to introduce over the past five years to cover their "blue-collar" service operations such as street cleaning, grounds maintenance, and so on. Reviews of the effects of this central government initiative (Walsh & Davis, 1993) suggest that there is now a better appreciation of the use of competition in local public services. What is less appreciated, however, is the potentially stultifying effect of this more quantitative, legalistic form of arranging working relations between those parts of the local authority (and outside contractors) that deliver the service. All too often, the tendering process has led to a "freezing" of work processes and performance standards at the level existing at the time of specification and letting of the contract. The result has been an emphasis, between the "client" and "contractor" parts of the organization, on competing for their "share of the fixed cake".

It is only recently that the value of developing services and improving standards of service delivery to customers *during the contract* has been recognized. Workshops with the chief executive and his senior officers helped highlight how the stress on quantification and procedures had led to an under-appreciation of the impact of context on performance and the damaging split of focus between the two arms of the organization. As part of a new "development agenda", commitments were made to start doing something about the quality of working relationships. During the second round of tendering now taking place, this more developmental perspective is having a positive impact on contract negotiations, and, in the words of the chief executive, "we are now looking at the feasibility of building non-quantitative cultural factors into the contract".

In our view, the control of complex social organizations is likely to be enhanced when the effect on individual and organization behaviour of an emphasis on quantitative measurement is better understood and there is a greater appreciation of the central but essentially unmeasurable contribution of many of our mental constructions to what we mean by "performance".

Once the consultant has had some success in helping immediate clients attend more consistently to feedback as they work through change, it becomes possible to consider moving up a level. This entails moving from a primary focus on the changes themselves, to the learning processes that are being used to achieve this. Here we can start to work on the challenging ideas of "learning to learn" and the "learning organization", aspirations that have been around for some time but are not yet widely understood or practised. At this level of working we come to the third shift in consulting stance which is about helping people in organizations become more conscious of and interested in developing their learning processes. This category is constituted by the remaining four of the "reframes" we have identified.

Reframe 7—From instructive to interactive

As with the top-down communication of vision and strategy, so too with much of the training provided to support implementation. The focus too often is on results, the "whats" that people are expected to carry out. This seems to be true even in programmes aimed at changing the culture, although some attempt is usually made to explicate the new behaviours required, through lists of the new values—the "hows"—that are required. However, these lists often seem to be regarded as just another set of "whats". This is a critical area where new policy needs to be translated into new practices.

The training methods used focus very much on the "knowledge" and "technical/professional" aspects of performance and seem to pay little attention to the contextual and relational dimensions of the practices—what we have started to call the "how of the how". In a recent discussion with the culture-change management team of a highly regarded information service, it became evident that this was the assumption being worked to. Journalist training was operating very much under its own direction, almost wholly disconnected from the intentions, strategies, and values guiding the thinking of the top team. In fact, according to one member of the team, they were hoping that "management" would continue to let them do their own thing! The idea that this training of journalists was one of *the* main means of inculcating the new culture, as much as improved writing and editing skills, just hadn't occurred to anybody. As a result of this thought, the group were quickly able to identify the requisite components of a "system to introduce new cultural practices" and to start to remedy the missing elements and communication links.

But this is not an unusual situation in large, hierarchical, multi-site organizations. It is very difficult to get the message across, particularly if it is a complex and unpopular one. We were rather struck a few months ago by an apparent paradox within one of our media clients. They clearly were working to an explicit policy of providing more "explanation" and less direct information in their output, in line with recent trends in the United States and here, for a "call to context". The way they were implementing a major change in organization and new working arrangements, however, provided a stark contrast to this. Most of the internal communication was top-down, one-way, and instructional, as though there was really no need at all to establish an agreed context with their staff and to explain the fundamental changes that were being pushed through. When this contradiction was pointed out to a very senior manager, he did acknowledge that "we do seem to have a bit of a communication problem here".

Large organizations do require special approaches to increase the speed and take-up of change. The training "cascade" concept (discussed in Reframe 5) has merit but appears to run out of steam very rapidly in culture-change programmes. In our view, these methods will work more effectively when they more explicitly address the need for *each* level in the hierarchy to *experience* the new thinking, to move from the enthusiastic *espousal* of new ideas to learning how to *enact* or live the new beliefs and values, and then, finally, to *enable* the next level down to work through this four-step process.

In our view, investment in training yields greater payback when new learning is distilled from personal experience and these ideas integrated with daily practices through trial application and adaptation to feedback. The translation of policy to practice represents a critical development hurdle, requiring that such training devotes explicit attention to the "how of the how" of new cultural practices.

Reframe 8—From instruments to processes of management

The search for "simple answers to complex problems" continues unabated in the field of management development. Here the idea of excellence in management, characterized by the possession of a generic list of "core competencies", dominates current thinking. In sympathy with the general trend towards behavioural theories of management, these lists focus very much on a range of individual "doing" skills—for example, negotiating, appraising, and so forth. There is often little sense of connection or coherence in these lists, and, as with our comments above on training, virtually no attention is paid to the contextual or relational aspects of these skills. Our experience of the effects of corporate communication and management-development programmes using this approach is not encouraging.

More recently, some writers, typically academics rather than commercial practitioners, have been critical of this universalistic approach and have started to point the way to a more relational view. For example, Morgan (1988) identifies "doing" skills, which are to do with the context and relations (e.g. "building bridges and alliances" or "managing multiple stakeholders"). Cave and McKeown (1993) talk about "higher-order capacities", like "reading the situation", "political acumen", and so forth, which are seen as prerequisites to the effective use of knowledge and skill. Hay (1990) focuses on "core characteristics" which are needed to deal with changes in context, such as "multiple perspectives". While these approaches do start to question the impact of context on competency, they leave open quite how this is to be accounted for in practical terms.

We have attempted to introduce a systemic frame when asked to introduce competencies into management processes of assessment, appraisal, and development. Our design of such assignments starts from a view that competencies describe *behaviour in relationships*, not individual behaviour in isolation. So competencies are mental constructs, things that arise through a process of negotiation and agreement between people. The meaning of these constructs is socially created through the process of people "agreeing that they are experiencing the same event (*activity*) in the same way" (Anderson

& Goolishian, 1988). Another lens we like to use sees competencies as constructs linked to theories that attempt to explain reality, and that as such they are constantly subject to revision, as experience is used to search for more useful ways of thinking about, describing, and working with systems. In this way, competencies equally can be seen as reflecting an ideology about management behaviour, invented by a dominant group at a moment in time for practical reasons. So even the constructs of competencies are not something fixed, but are products of a process, an evolving attempt to find better theories to guide actions.

We used this frame of process, rather than instrument, when we worked with a division of a major public development agency that wanted to use competencies to establish a more objective basis for selecting, appraising, and rewarding staff. The client felt that this approach of surfacing competency constructs grounded in their local practices was a better alternative (on the grounds of greater face validity) than the use of generic master lists of competencies produced by surveys and norming across a range of industries.

We pushed closer to the relational and process end of our continuum by testing these constructs internally using focus groups of staff, and externally through conversations with clients of the agency about their perceptions of effective behaviour seen in some agency staff compared with others. The final component of our process approach required staff to use these constructs in regular meetings and twice-yearly performance appraisal reviews. By linking the performance management process to strategic planning, we created the potential for feedback upwards as well as inwards from forces outside the client system, to inform the consensus about the utility of these initial constructs. As strategic needs and local performance changed, so managers and staff could refine the competencies they regarded as useful, constantly drawing the use of these constructs away from the instrumental and towards the process end of our spectrum.

In our view, constructs such as management competencies become more useful when they are seen as relational and continually evolving, as a result of a dialogue across system subcomponents about the means by which understanding and the performance of the system can be improved.

Reframe 9—From literal to oral communications

Talk to managers in an organization going through change, and they will say, to a person, that there is a desperate need for "more communication". Staff become anxious about the future, and gossip and rumour-mongering flourish as small groups all over the organization try to make sense of all the little individual bits of "data" that they see around them; for example, an awayday for the top team, a change in stock levels, visits from consultants, and so on. What surprises us, then, is that in most organizations just the opposite seems to take place when change is in the air. Any pools of effective communication processes that might exist just seem to dry up, and even managers who are known as good communicators get completely overwhelmed in special corporate performance audits and ever more meetings as top management prepare their strategy, plans, and communications.

We came across a particular illustration of this phenomenon while working with a European media organization that was in the process of decentralizing and introducing new performance-management disciplines. While running a series of events for senior output staff, we were made aware that many previously "hands-on" managers of the individual services had become increasingly distant from staff and the core output. This had resulted in a position in some areas where there was almost a complete breakdown of trust and real communication between the "management" and "production", with the only genuine dialogue being "in-group" rather than between the groups. When (in the relative safety of these development events) staff questioned the long "silences" that seemed to follow the odd general announcement, a frequent management response was: "Well, we can't tell people things we don't yet know, or haven't finally decided on."

This way of thinking about communication, and the resulting sense of alienation, is an example of the model of communication that most managers now seem to hold, what Ong (1982) calls the "pipeline" or media model of communication. In this view, communications are very much one-way, self-reflexive, and free-standing "packages" of facts (e.g. briefing notes, chief executive videos, noticeboard materials, etc.), which are sent along a "pipeline" to the various recipients throughout the organization. Not only does this medium "strip the context" from the message, thereby making it difficult for the receivers to understand what is meant, but it also alienates the receivers. Clearly this is an instance where the analogic dimension of McLuhan's "the medium is the message" carries the most weight, and the corporate intention to clarify, reorientate, and motivate usually gets completely distorted. As Watzlawick has pointed out (Watzlawick et al., 1974), the solution has become the problem.

It seems that the "technologizing" of the word (Ong, 1982) that has taken place in the late twentieth century has almost wholly overwhelmed our oral heritage. We now feel most comfortable with a more literary perspective on communication, whether it is in the form of the printed word or in the "secondary orality" (Ong, 1982) of modern media like radio and television. While there have been tremendous gains from this shift, there have been important losses, particularly in larger systems where the dimension of context that is inherent in the oral tradition has been lost. What the "pipeline" model lacks is the "intersubjectivity" of the oral or human model of communication. In this mode, managers need to be able to *anticipate the feedback* in order to communicate. That is, they need to have a sense of the context(s) into which they are speaking, in order to communicate.

When managers and staff have face to face opportunities to complete what Barnett Pearce calls the **conversational triplet** (see Glossary), the context can be foregrounded: people can check the particular meaning of conversations they are having and, at the same time, refine and reaffirm the frames they are implicitly using to guide the dialogue.

It seems to us that the popularity of the management technique MBWA [managing by walking about] has its roots in this perspective. How else than by talking informally with staff in their places of work are managers able to appreciate the many differ-

ences that characterize the local contexts inhabited by different groups of workers? And how else can the two-way communication that follows have a chance of taking place within what Ken Gergen has called a "local ontology" in which "universal" and "local" ideas can be related? Unfortunately, the MBWA technique has, for many organizations undergoing change, remained a good idea that has yet to be translated into practice, and the benefits of the oral tradition see the light of day only in special development events.

Reframe 10—From espousal to enactment

Our position as constructionist consultants is that change is an ongoing process, not a thing that can be specified as a fixed target. Take empowerment as an example. This is a construct that is given meaning only when people can agree on what they experience in common. Top management may agree amongst themselves what they want to happen by focusing on this concept as a theme for change. But as soon as the communication or change cascade starts, the meaning of the concept will begin to be influenced by meanings that people lower down make of the idea from *their* context of experience. Management may, by the pressure of the communication effort, succeed in privileging a certain definition of empowerment in words and processes, but the behaviour that they will see will always reflect the mediation of the experiences of the rest of the organization upon the intent of the leadership group.

According to work done by Garfinkel (1967), the taken-for-granted social skills we use to negotiate our way through our daily routine are in fact skilful accomplishments. Furthermore, Weick's associated concept of *enactment* (1979) suggests that we actively structure our social realities, though through a largely unconscious process. New practices can therefore be regarded as essentially new *cultural* practices, requiring attention to issues of context, relationships, and dynamics, as well as of behaviour. Experience of a range of client consultations leads us to suggest that if the cascading of new values in action is to succeed, there has to be some enactment, requiring change at three levels:

1. within the leadership;
2. in the relationship between the leadership and the rest of staff;
3. in the cultural context in which they all operate.

To illustrate this, at one of the major clearing banks, a senior manager was sufficiently intrigued by our written start of a conversation about change implementation to continue a dialogue with us from which a very different approach emerged. There were a number of issues that the client manager thought connected with what he described as "our type of consultancy". There were then a number of false starts: conversations begun with colleagues where our approach did not fit with their expectations of consultants, or where the positivist role-idea of these managers made them uncomfortable with what seemed a rather under-specified consulting process. Finally, however, a conversation was started about the difficulty of introducing new ideas about the long-term management of purchasing which had been produced by an internal O&M study group.

We talked about the range of people who would be affected by the introduction of this new policy and the range of initiatives already started, building up a map of the system of people who were all talking about finding different ways of lowering the ratio of actual costs to budget. We had an idea of working with this *whole* group. This was a very different approach for defining policy, but one that seemed to fit the range of unformed proposals and wide range of stakeholders. We moved on to look at the client's goal. It was nothing less than the "buy-in" by this wide range of stakeholders to a new way of thinking about purchasing. We discussed the alternatives of "instruction" and "discovery" as a way of changing people's ideas. This helped to expose a dilemma. The study group's report had already been put forward to senior management and approved. However, if this chunk of policy were put forward to the "problem system" as proposals to be "understood" and accepted, management knew that they would not get the quality of buy-in that they needed.

The resolution to that dilemma that emerged from our conversation was to take a step back now in order to move forward faster at a later time. The hypothesis that was accepted was: that the system would buy-in to the new idea of purchasing management with greater ownership and commitment, if the ideas already formed by the study team were seen as only a starting point, set out for amendment or radical rethinking by "the system". The client manager accepted the systemic concept of **equifinality** (see Glossary) and abandoned the instructive interaction model.

In our view, complex change is more surely implemented when espousal of new ideas is followed by the enactment of new behaviours, within the leadership, in the relationship between the leadership and the rest of staff, and in the cultural context in which they all operate, so that the whole organization begins to experience itself as behaving differently and making new meaning from their interactions with each other and the external environment.

SUMMARY

From these ten reframes (which are certainly not in any sense "commandments"), we can draw certain conclusions about the criteria that systemic consultation in large organizations needs to address if it is to be both acceptable and effective. Our first appreciation of this new "ology" is summarized below.

	Frame shift	Suggested benefits
1.	Universal to local	Policies and programmes become meaningful when opportunity is created for interaction between corporate intent and local practice
2.	Observed to observing systems	Adaptiveness and flexibility of systems are enhanced when change agents connect their own previous and anticipated actions to the problems of change and "resistance"
3.	Part to whole	Including a broader representation of the system in policy formulation leads to more radical change and higher commitment levels from system members

4.	Debate to dialogue	Letting go of habitual debating patterns for a more relativist position expressed through dialogical inquiry brings forth greater awareness of other options for change, and other explanations that dis-solve problems
5.	Detail to dynamic complexity	Change leadership becomes more effective when it switches from a focus on the detailing of processes to managing meaning using feedback arising from the dynamics of the change process
6.	Quantification to appreciation	The control of complex social organizations is enhanced when the effect on individual and organization behaviour of an emphasis on quantitative measurement is understood, and there is a greater appreciation of the central but essentially unmeasurable contribution of many of our mental constructs to what we mean by performance.
7.	Instructive to interactive	Training investment yields greater payback when new learning is distilled from experience and the results integrated with daily practice through trial application and adaptation to feedback
8.	Instruments to processes of management	Constructs become more useful when seen as continually evolving from a dialogue across the system about means for improving understanding and performance
9.	Literacy to orality	The complexity of the impact of local situations on change prescriptions is best handled in face-to-face communication, reflecting the contexting strengths of the oral tradition

10.	Espousal to enactment	Complex change is more surely implemented when espousal of new ideas is followed by the enactment of new behaviours, within the leadership, in the relationship between the leadership and the rest of staff, and in the cultural context in which they all operate

From these experiences, we have evolved a hybrid consulting style in our work with large organizations, to deal with the differences between using these ideas with small groups and within organizations.

The greatest difference is often getting to the consultation, where in "selling" assignments the task of gaining acceptance of the need for this particular form of help is much more difficult. We are currently developing a range of approaches within which we find we can be "systemic enough", but which also help us tackle the selling problem. We illustrate these approaches in the three cases that follow in Chapters 3, 4, and 5, and in the final three chapters on methodology and identity.

PART II

PRAXIS—
THE CONSTRUCTIONIST
APPROACH
IN ACTION

"The way to solve the problem you see in life is to live in
a way that will make what is problematic disappear."

Wittgenstein

CHAPTER 3

A Board-level consultation

Using the design process
to develop a reflexive capability

What do systemic practitioners and constructionist consultants do when they are faced with offering consultation to clients in situations that are new to them, not only technically but culturally, and clearly involve high risk—to the clients if things go wrong, and to the practitioners themselves in terms of reputation and personal confidence? This chapter describes the design and running of an "awayday" event for the board of directors of a new NHS Trust hospital. It explores some of the important issues that are raised when a new group involving executives from the private and public sectors first come together to clarify the key principles that are to govern the operation of a highly visible public service unit. As the first of the three cases in Part II, it illustrates how during the early stages of development of a systemic way of working, consultants can usefully apply systemic thinking to plan and design strategic and development events. This systemic design process helps consultants develop a contingency capability for handling potentially difficult situations and a variety of possible outcomes.

T his enquiry came to me through a long-standing client with whom I had been working for about a year. During one of our discussions he said that a close friend had recently been appointed as Chairman of one of the new NHS Trust hospitals. He had just completed appointing his new Board and was looking for some outside assistance to help set up and run an awayday to get the executive and non-executive directors together for the first time, "To make a start on strategy and action plans for the team".

Although I had very little work experience in the NHS, I was not overly concerned about my lack of direct knowledge of the "content" of the client's work. The focus (and consequently, the added value of the systemic adviser) is usually on the aspects of "context" and "process" that give the content meaning. This perspective would allow me to consider the effects of my actions as information or feedback (rather than error), using this to understand afresh the meaning that people were placing on the action, and hence to get a sense of the context(s) they were working from.

So, instead of trying to become an overnight expert on the Trust concept, I tried rather to identify the basic questions that would inform my first discussion with him. I found myself wondering why he felt he needed outside help with this meeting, particularly from someone who was outside the NHS system. Did he have some doubts about his ability to connect with and carry the non-executives from industry? Or were there some sensitivities involving the existing executive directors, and possibly some difficulties with the NHS establishment?

AGREEING THE ASSIGNMENT

The Chairman proved to be charming but with the pragmatic results-orientation of the experienced politician. He was frank about the situation he was facing, his particular goals and concerns for the awayday, and what he was looking for from the external helper.

• How to weld together the new Board team of existing NHS executive directors and the new non-executives who were from outside the NHS and had little direct experience of the operation; the three executives had already been brought together by the experience of developing the mission for the hospital and applying for Trust status. Was there likely to be some difficulty in reopening the debate to allow the non-executives on board?

• How to maintain a sense of continuity for existing staff, while taking advantage of the transition to Trust status to introduce the new thinking and practices required to deliver "more from less".

• How to clarify the "fundamentals" (i.e. vision, strategy, and values) that the new team could cohere around—which could take some time given the disparate nature of the group—while building early credibility for the new team through prioritizing and taking action over the first six months on the most important elements of work for the Board.

He was hoping by means of this event to set up various arrangements to give the new group and himself some structure to work to, and to build a greater sense of solidarity.

As I had surmised, he seemed a little nervous of the "business" aspects of the new situation which he and his executive colleagues had not had to deal with before. This anxiety was amplified by the uncertainty arising from the difficulties that he and the Chief Executive seemed to be having. Was this perhaps the reason for choosing someone to help who was not part of the NHS establishment and who also was used to dealing with interpersonal conflict?

The working hypothesis that I would use to guide my initial thinking about the awayday event went as follows:

• The Chairman seemed to fear a major split developing between the two constituent parts of the new Board: the full-time, long-serving, and battle-hardened executives, and the new external appointees who knew little of the operation and who would only ever spend a comparatively small amount of time on Trust business.

- I sensed that this factor heightened his concerns about the relationship with the Chief Executive, which was effectively the key to Board integration. The Chairman had prior experience of the NHS and a desire to "lead from the front", and he was expected to put in three full days a week at the hospital. The Chief Executive had been at the hospital for some time and seemed to be in a strong position given his achievement in steering the Trust application to success. The potential for conflict was high, and I wondered if this might be leading to a certain tentativeness in their dealings with each other, which could be hindering the development of more open communications and closer working relations in the wider group.

- As a result, I had the impression that he was looking to the new non-executive directors for help in creating a context in which this relationship could be redefined and become a better basis for effective working at all levels.

If my hypothesis was correct, the likely focus of the awayday would need to be very much on creating a context in which the issue of *working relations* could be explored. I decided that though the Chairman was keen to influence *behaviour* between Board members, this event would need to focus more on the *network of relations* within and around the Board. It would therefore need to be designed to work at the level of *identity*—that is, "Who are we as a Board, who am I as a director, and who am I as a person creating a new type of organization in the NHS?" Useful discussions at this level would provide a container or frame for other developments in knowledge and capability—and hence behaviour (which might take some time to take effect). My outline proposal was therefore framed with this very much as the central theme.

From a social constructionist perspective, what is actually meant by behaviour is not a matter of scientific fact—that is, something to be "discovered"—but rather a matter of "negotiation" between all the participants in the situation. When people first meet, this construction process often seems to be influenced most strongly by participants' sense of identity—hence my hunch that this was the level to focus on at this moment in time.

Calling a few days later, I was very pleased to hear that he liked the proposal I had put forward. We talked about the next stage, which was to be a series of initial interviews with his Board colleagues. We both felt that it was crucial that I established some kind of rapport with the directors before the actual event. Because of time pressures on the non-executives, my conversations with them would have to be over the telephone, but I would visit the hospital to meet all the executives face to face. We also agreed that I would attend the next Board meeting to get an idea of how they were working together.

PREPARING FOR THE AWAYDAY

Now that I had the assignment, my next step would be to make contact with the other members of the Board. I already had a feeling that this would not be without problems, particularly with the non-executives, who were all high-profile people, with very busy lives outside their hospital commitments. I thought it would be best to start with the four executives (Chief Executive, Finance Director, Medical Director, and Nursing Director), as they were likely to be more grounded and accessible. Meeting them a few days later made a big difference to my own frame of mind as I became more grounded myself. My fantasies based on the Chairman's pen pictures were brought down to earth as I started to connect with the actual people I was to work with and to identify how they were understanding the situation.

The four executives formed a very mixed group, and I could see why the Chairman might be having some difficulties in relating to them. The Chief Executive and Finance Director were both very rational and businesslike in manner, acutely aware of the financial dangers the Trust was in, and rather dismissive of the contribution the non-executives would be able to make. The Chief Executive made it clear that while he respected the Chairman, he was rather worried about his rather expansive vision for the hospital, and how this was encouraging the "wrong kind of expectations" within the medical fraternity—for example, a "go for growth" spirit. He was also worried that this might give the non-executives the wrong "expansionist" ideas leading to immediate conflict over future policy.

The two executives with medical responsibilities came across in a rather different fashion and seemed much more connected to the original values of the NHS. We had what seemed to be a more even-handed discussion about the difficulties the organization was facing, in that both the aspirations and the cost constraints were given an equal voice in our conversations. They were clearly less close to the Chief Executive and quite sympathetic to the Chairman's intentions, with the Medical Director quite outspoken in his criticisms of the policies that were being followed by the hospital in order to maintain financial viability.

The conversations with the non-executives proved to be far less enlightening. I was unable to contact one who was out of the country until the day of the awayday, and the others were, quite understandably, guarded in their comments over the phone. The general sense I got was one of uncertainty about role, perceived ignorance about the NHS, and concern about how they were going to build relations with the executives given their own limited availability. I was disappointed to learn that the only non-executive who had NHS experience was ill and unlikely to be able to attend—I had been seeing her as offering one potential link between the executives and non-executives.

I was very glad that I had put the time in to meet the directors and talk to most of the non-executives and would not be meeting them for the first time on the day. The effectiveness of outside facilitation depends very much on the quality of relationship the outsider enjoys with the participants, and leaving that to the day is risky. It also puts too much pressure on the facilitator at the start of the event, just when he or she should be wholly focused on the business at hand.

Though the interviews had been disappointing in some respects, they had provided much food for thought and had influenced the way I was now thinking about the "system" I was engaged with. My initial working hypothesis clearly had to be extended to take account of:

- The distance between the executives and non-executives, which seemed wider than I had originally thought. The non-executives felt uncertain and ill at ease with their new roles, and seemed to have built few connections with the hospital so far; their lack of availability was just one indication of how busy they were, as was their concern at having to spend more than half a day a month on hospital business. I found it difficult to see how they would have the confidence and grasp to play the strong integrating role that the Chairman was looking for, particularly as the executives seemed quite sceptical of the benefits they would bring.

• The splitting was not just between executive and non-executive. The interviews with the executives indicated that there were further differences between the "medicals" and the "administrators" of a quite significant nature. These differences were being polarized by the group of medical consultants who saw the arrival of the new Chairman as an opportunity to change the current rather stringent policy on new medical developments. This was leading to suspicion over motives between the two and was probably a greater source of tension between the Chairman and the Chief Executive than the arrival of the non-executives.

• The concept of **multiple realities** (see Glossary) had been brought home to me with this group: the non-executives knew very little about each other or their executive colleagues, and there were differences in this latter group. The Board members as a whole clearly had a long way to go before they could establish any of the sort of shared thinking about vision, roles, and policies that they would need to operate in a cohesive way. It was clear already that *connectedness* was going to be one of the main issues, and providing opportunities to identify and establish new relations would need to be a key feature of the design of the process for the awayday.

• The difficulties in the relationship between the Chairman and Chief Executive were clearly not just about different styles. They also represented different poles of a basic dilemma facing these new Trusts as they sought to improve performance: the need to introduce a stronger cost-control–orientated "management" culture to ensure that scarce resources were used to the best advantage; as against the desire to use a more "entre-preneurial" approach to bring in the fresh new ideas and crea-tive thinking that the Trust would need to improve overall effectiveness. So at a higher level the event was also very much about the discourse in the wider society about how the NHS should be managed.

- In addition to the earlier focus on "relationships", I thought that it would now also be important to work on developing an **ecology of ideas** (see Glossary)—that set of concepts and prin-ciples that would guide the strategic thinking of this group. It was also clear to me that people were quite anxious and tense about this first event ("Is it going to be like group psycho-therapy?") and people were looking to me much more to pro-vide "a safe pair of hands" and a sense of protection, as they started to deal with the difficulties they sensed would surface during the event.

DESIGNING THE PROCESS

Systemic work requires that the practitioner pays close attention to the actual flow of communication and meaning, *as it happens*. How-ever, it is possible to build in through the design process a series of activities and experiences that are more likely to lead participants into the "observer position" and hence into the new perspectives that might initiate change. This is particularly valuable for both the novice and solo systemic practitioner, as it can take some of the pressure off being "all-seeing" during the event itself. It also can help develop versatility and a capability to deal with unforeseen contingencies. Given my lack of experience in this particular arena, I realized that it was important to make full use of the design phase to improve my chances of dealing in an effective way with the issues and problems that might arise during the event.

By this stage my mind was working overtime and the ideas for the event were bubbling up. There was time for about six sessions over the night and day, which could be used to provide a sequence of steps to guide and develop the thinking of the group, ending up with some action planning. The following was the overall flow of activities that I eventually settled on.

During the Friday evening:

Session 1: Setting the Context.   Developing a shared map of the key issues that members feel are likely to affect the setting up and development of the Trust. This work would be very participative in order to stimulate interaction and full contributions from all.

My intention here was to use the fishbowl format to encourage both subgroups—i.e. executive and non-executive—to talk "insider language" when in the fishbowl, and to focus on listening to the others when outside it.

Session 2: Grounding the discussion.   Over dinner and aided by an informal presentation by a senior speaker from the NHS, reviewing the earlier views from Session 1 in the light of aims, objectives, and constraints at NHS level.

My intention here was to provide an opportunity for the Board (especially the non-executives) to start making connections to the wider context, perhaps making a different sense of the issues they had brought to the surface earlier.

[Informal discussion after dinner]

During the Saturday morning:

Session 3: Finding a starting point.   Both groups (executive and non-executive) would separately identify and share their thoughts and feelings on: "The values, ideas, and practices I want/intend to bring into the new Trust". This would serve to alert people to important beliefs held and areas of common interest, as well as potential conflicts. It would also start to reduce the underlying anxiety that people might be feeling about what they might have to give up or change to work in this group.

My intention here was to help the group settle a little by getting them to discover the areas where they held common views; I also thought this would be a good way to surface in a non-threatening way some of the important differences that might exist at a beliefs level. I thought we might use the fishbowl format again, but just for the report back.

Session 4: Creating a desired future.   Building on the core values identified in Session 3, the group would work to create a shared sense of what kind of Trust hospital the Board would hope to develop: i.e. its vision, in relation to its raison d'être—i.e. its mission—as a provider of services in the area.

My intention here was to get the Board members to translate the beliefs and values they had identified into practices so that everybody could start to experience in more concrete terms what they were think- ing about. I thought we could use here the idea of a "stakeholder" network: after the group had identified the key stakeholders, they could attempt to have "dialogues" with each of them about how the hospital would be expressing the vision in practice.

[Lunch]

During Saturday afternoon:

Session 5: Identifying a strategy for change.   Following an identification of the key issues/gaps/blockages that need to be addressed to deliver the "governing ideas" developed in Session 4, the Board would work in two or three small groups to develop possible ways forward on the central challenges facing the organization. A review of the proposals developed in this session would provide the strategic framework that would guide Board decision-making during the first six months of the Trust's existence.

I was thinking of using a "systems sculpt" [a way of physically modelling how people experience their relatedness] here to identify the different groupings that were "in the group mind", before the small group work started. I was hoping that by this stage participants would not form on the basis solely of executive vs. non-executive groupings, but would have been able to identify a number of different bases for alignments/alliances—e.g. links with the teaching side, investment in facilities to attract private patients, empowerment of staff, etc. I also thought that this might provide for the "subgroups" that had formed an interesting opportunity to exchange "expectations" of each other while sitting in the sculpt, rather than across a boardroom table. If time permitted I thought we might also explore any dilemmas that were revealed by the sculpting process—e.g. "how to be loyal to the idea of

*an open accident/emergency service while also supporting the develop-
ment of specialist elective surgery services."*

Session 6: Formulating an initial action plan.   In this final part of
the event the focus would become increasingly practical, with
the Board committing themselves singly and in different
groupings to carrying out the first steps required to move the
strategic work forward. These decisions would be documented
and would form the Board's first formal action plan. Time
permitting, each major action would be reviewed in the light of
likely reactions and feedback from interested parties, in order to
use the combined experience of Board members to build in
contingency planning where appropriate. The last activity of the
day would focus on the learning that members had got out of
the event and would build a feeling of more integration within
the group.

*After a period of exploration and reflection we think that it is
important that groups take the time to translate ideas and general
proposals into specific and concrete action plans. For most of us the
important signifier of meaning is action ". . . we place more value on
what people do than what they say". My thought here was to start off
with a review session to crystallize thinking and set priorities reasonably quickly. The time could then be focused on working through a few
key pieces of action that would give the group a sense of achievement at
the end of the event, and help the Chairman and Chief Executive play
out how they saw their own roles as we moved from policy to implementation.*

* * *

*I was excited by the flow and coherence of this design and the possibilities
it offered for working at several levels and so getting more leverage (i.e.
extra mileage) out of exercises I had used before (e.g. the stakeholder
discussions and the system sculpt). The important point to emphasize here
is that for the inexperienced practitioner who is working alone in a difficult situation, it is possible to build in a certain amount of reflexivity,
both for himself and for the group as a whole. By using systemic principles
to design the flow of work and the specific exercises used, it becomes
possible for the facilitator to favour more the role of an "orchestrator" of
various conversations rather than that of a "hands on" expert who is
expected to offer pronouncements and push things along.*

Through the design process it is also possible to build a certain degree of "redundancy" (multiple possible options) into the event itself. This can give you the added confidence that you need to work flexibly as you are more likely to have the "requisite variety" to fit the demands of the emerging situation. In practice, these two ideas help me work more intuitively in response to on-going feedback once the event has started, in line with the dictum "don't plan much beyond the first opportunity for feedback".

I was, however, rather worried about the time available and felt that in practice I would have to think about what activities I could leave out or cut short—it would depend very much on the way the discussions were developing and what people seemed to want most as the event progressed.

I recognize now that workshops like this seldom turn out as you had intended, once the planned sequence of activities interacts with the "real world" brought in by the participants. The mind-map that you, the consultant, had developed with the main sponsor always differs somewhat from the maps brought by others. Even prior interviewing, although helpful for developing working hypotheses, cannot replace the value of comparing peoples' mental maps in real-time interaction. This is when the normally invisible process of social construction (see Chapter 1) becomes most visible, both to the consultant and the insiders themselves.

RUNNING THE AWAYDAY

First evening—orientation

Several people turned up late and were quite surprised that we were going to work before supper (it *was* a Friday). So, after a brief introduction to the event I went straight into the fishbowl exercise, deciding that if the executives went first it would "anchor" our discussions. The question I set them was: "What are the challenges facing the hospital, and what do the non-executives need to understand about this?" A few flippant remarks were made suggesting that going into a fishbowl was unnecessary, but once they sat down and started talking in the circle of seats I had put out, the discussion took off. Almost immediately the divisions within the executive group became apparent, but in addition, and in contrast, it appeared that there was also quite a strong consensus on a range of other issues that were seen as problematic:

- the new "care consortia" management organization was not really working effectively, with the managers and clinicians often clashing;
- there was too much focus on the "cuts/savings" mentality, and a felt need to reframe these discussions as being about "effectiveness";
- there was a concern about the way "the competition" had got their "houses (and cost levels) in order", and their clinicians "on board".

There seemed to be a genuine shared concern about the future and the need to make changes. After about twenty minutes, I suggested that the groups should swap around and the non-executives now have their own discussion but to relate it to what they had just heard: "What have you picked up . . . any surprises, etc., and what do you think the Board has to focus on now?" They found this a little difficult, but in the end managed to identify a number of issues that they saw as important:

- they didn't want to be seen as "rubber stampers" and were worried as to how they could take up more effective positions, given their lack of direct experience—e.g. they noted that the care consortia issue had not even appeared on a Board agenda as yet, or the role to be played by a medical school that the hospital had links with;
- there were clear difficulties in having good discussions on the "beds vs. budget" issues: there was little trust and ineffective mechanisms for resolving differences in what seemed to be a "spiritual conflict";
- one of the non-executives, a board director in a large private-sector organization, noted that in their boardroom there was "only one leader" and the "facts" were a lot less contentious; although the hospital had successfully got to the Trust stage, it was less clear how it was to move in a more integrated way into an uncertain future.

Because dinner was approaching, I decided to leave out a short input on "the role of the director", and to finish off with two quick exercises: a brief open reflection on the two discussions; and a statement from each person as to what they now wanted to achieve by the end of the awayday.

The open reflection (in response to: "What issues are likely to form the strongest links between you?") led to some very useful comments from both sides: "There was a lack of definition of 'vision' . . . the non-executives were hung up about this, and felt 'guilty' about operations . . . whereas the executives were guilty about the vision, and hung up about operations . . . the non-executives were surprised by the morale problems and the difficulties with the clinicians, and wondered how they could get more in touch . . . the Trust represented 'good news' for many, so how does one get a more positive approach to the opportunities? . . ."

Reflection activity is a very important part of our approach and serves several purposes: it provides a "punctuation" after a period of action, allowing people to think about what they've done and what it means to them; this puts them in an "observer position" to their experience, which helps them appreciate the context in which they are acting and get a different, "outside-in" perspective on their action; finally, it gives people an opportunity to connect this experience to others they have had, to draw conclusions, and to generalize—i.e. to learn from their experience.

The round robin on desired outcomes that followed produced a strong consensus on the need to "get everybody on board" at all levels, and to find ways of using the outside perspective that the non-executives could offer. The general sense was that this opening exercise had broken the ice and made a number of new connections between individuals, and people went in to supper feeling a little more positive than when they had arrived.

The morning after—identifying the issues

In the morning I thought I should put a "positive frame" on the previous evening's work, and I talked a little about "A lot more on the table . . . differences expressed . . . no walking wounded . . .

differences not just along executive/non executive lines . . . offering clues to other linkages . . . and so on." I thought they now needed some kind of "umbrella" idea to contain and orientate the debate—perhaps not yet *the* "vision", but an ongoing dialogue out of which the direction would emerge, not only for them but for others who were not in the room. Prior to looking at this in more detail, we did another quick review to pick up any thoughts people had had following the over-dinner discussion. What came out very clearly from this quick snapshot was an anxiety to look at the finances of the business and "get down to some *practical* discussion".

The idea of putting a positive frame on something is an important one. There were many interpretations that could be put on the previous night's work. Each interpretation would depend on how the interpreter was understanding the context, an important aspect of which would be their expectations. For people who have not had much experience of working in this way, the process can seem slow and chaotic, as people struggle to make sense of the wide variety of perceptions and interests. Positively connoting the experience takes the pressure off people to impose order too soon, to force consensus when it is not there, and so on. It encourages people not to feel guilty, defend, or justify, but to accept their experience and explore what it might mean.

I decided to delay the planned "vision" session and give the Finance Director an immediate slot to explain how the balance sheet looked and how the NHS finance system worked—they would be unable to focus on the future if they were too much in the dark about the financial present. While this brief interim session seemed both to interest and confuse the non-executives a little (how *does* public finance really work?), it also seemed to settle the group a little—we were now dealing with the "hard facts" from which everything else flowed!

This change of plan illustrates very well what is probably the primary principle of systemic working: "follow the feedback". Although we needed to get started on the vision, the group were clearly worried about the "finances". If I had ignored this "message", it is highly likely that the

quality of connection between us, and consequently between them and the
event, would start to erode. I had needed to put my original design to one
side and follow this new lead for the moment to see where it led.

I then decided it was time to address the earlier question about vision. Given the group's expressed desire to be practical, I thought we would use *specific cases* that they thought pointed to the key dilemmas facing them. We brainstormed for ten minutes or so and then picked two issues that seemed to illustrate different aspects of the central problem: (1) was the hospital to offer a range of specialized elective services, and perhaps make more of existing connections with a medical school; or (2) was it to be a straightforward district general hospital dealing with acute and emergency work coming from the local community?

We often ask people to work on specific cases from their own work
experience when tackling more abstract questions of strategy and policy.
This is the special value of the "example"—it is an illustration of some-
thing that is both general and specific. This allows it to form a bridge
between matters of general policy and particular problems. When these
examples come directly from people's experiences/work situations, the
process allows them to learn about both theory and its practical applica-
tion, in other words to develop their own **praxis** *(see Glossary)*

The first case concerned the relations of the hospital to a medical school; and the second covered ways of raising clinician productivity in order to improve bed utilization. I asked the group to form two syndicates which in their view used the resources of the Board to the full. Initially they wanted to duck this decision, asking me to form the groups; but when I demurred, they did sort out two balanced groupings with a good mix between executive and non-executive. The most interesting choice was putting the non-executive with medical-school connections with the Chief Executive: they had been quite critical of each other's views up to this point, and so it was encouraging that they chose to confront their differences at this stage. I gave both groups an hour to work out some proposals for presentation after morning coffee.

Both groups really got stuck into the problems, clearly appreciating the shift from abstract and macro-level discussions to the more concrete. After coffee, we regrouped and took the presentations. What was both surprising and pleasing was the degree of consensus that seemed to emerge around the vision from the two rather different topics. It was becoming clear that a lot of the apparent conflict was in the way different people were **languaging** (see Glossary) the issues—and the more concrete examples had helped to dispel some of the confusion. So quite quickly the group was able to frame a general statement of the vision.

To test the robustness of their consensus, I first asked the group to identify all the important stakeholders who would have to buy into this vision. This led to a very interesting discussion for the group, who had, I think, got rather caught up in their own inner world. They were quite surprised by the number of stakeholders they had to satisfy and concerned at the likely conflicts that were inherent in such a diverse group. I then suggested that they tested their newly drafted vision by "talking" to a few of the more important stakeholders about the vision, and dealing with the kinds of comments such people were likely to make.

This involved them in spontaneously creating the kinds of conversations they might hold with particular interest groups—for example, the public, the NHS Executive, local newspapers, and so on—imagining the types of responses and reactions they might get and then dealing with those responses. This exercise in the social construction of reality really "sorted the sheep from the goats", and only the Chairman seemed able to "speak" the vision, imagine how these people would react, and respond effectively. The group found this to be a rather powerful indicator of their state of readiness as far as the vision was concerned. Despite encouragement, the group decided not to attempt to "talk through" such a conversation with the clinicians—a clear sign of a problem ahead, as this was seen to be one of the most important and difficult stakeholder groups!

This exercise provided a very good opportunity for the group to engage actively in the process of reality construction. The vision that they were starting to cohere around would only gain energy and currency—i.e. become privileged as an acceptable construction of events—when it was being appropriately languaged with the key stakeholders. The purpose of these "conversations with stakeholders" was to help this group start to

*explore the appropriate language that "made sense" to these others. Once
this form of language became a feature of the network of stakeholder
dialogues on a day-to-day basis, it was likely that this view of purpose
would be widely accepted as* **the** *view, the reality.*

We were very close to lunch by this stage, and so we did another
quick review to capture where people were and also what the
priorities were for the final afternoon. The main topic of interest
seemed to be around roles, in particular those of the Chairman and
the Chief Executive.

*I had been intending to ask them to exchange "expectations", in order
to encourage more specificity in the discussion of roles on the Board.
When this is done during the early stages of team formation, it helps both
individuals and the group to start building up and negotiating a shared
map of "who does what" from the perspective of interaction and relationships—in other words, dynamically, in contrast to the more typical static
job-description approach. It also establishes the norm that open discussions and negotiations about roles are important and legitimate activities.*

*But as time was now short, I decided that we needed to approach the
issue about roles raised by the pre-lunch discussion more directly by
starting with the relationship between the Chairman and the Chief Executive, in the context of the difficulties over direction and leadership that had
been evident during the earlier sessions. During these, there had been
much "proxy skirmishing" around these difficulties but very little direct
dialogue between these two key figures. The Chief Executive had been
very quiet in most sessions, and the challenge to his approach and views
had been carried mainly by one of the non-executives and the Medical
Director. My hunch was that in these last sessions, both groups would
now back away from confronting the difficulties in the leadership relationship (and their own cohesion as a Board) unless the two central figures
were given an opportunity to "show their true colours" before the meeting
ended. My role would be to enable this to happen without anybody getting
"damaged".*

The final afternoon—confronting the difficulties

After a quiet lunch during which most people were in reflective
mood, we started on the final session of the event. I talked a little

about the identified need for a more cohesive approach from the Board—whether this existed or not would be most obvious in the relations between the Chairman and the Chief Executive. I said I was going to ask the two of them to say something about how they saw their respective roles and the relationship. But first I wanted the other directors to have a conversation in which they identified their concerns and expectations individually and as a group: "What do you as a group expect from the leadership of the hospital?"

The group had by now reached a state where they were able to be quite frank about their views. The resulting discussion was not only lively but often blunt to the point of rudeness, despite the fact that the two leaders were sitting in their midst.

This is one of the real benefits of the fishbowl format, because the listeners do not respond and are in a sense eavesdropping; it is therefore possible for them to hear the conversation as observers, in a less defensive way, and this seems to encourage straight talking from the people in the fishbowl.

At one point I had to intervene as some of the remarks about the Chief Executive were getting rather personal, and the sympathy of the group seemed to be shifting very much in the direction of the Chairman. To encourage the group to adopt a different "non-blaming" approach to the difficulties, I pointed out that up until six months before, the Chief Executive had been seen as a hero as he battled to get the Trust application through. Now, all of a sudden, although still displaying the same "heroic" behaviour of earlier times, he was being cast as the bogeyman. What sense did this make . . . and were his strengths and values no longer of any importance to the hospital? This seemed to alter the quality of the conversation, and the group shifted the angle to talk more about the qualities they were looking for *from the function* rather than from particular individuals.

This is an important type of intervention particularly when emotions rise and people start blaming others for the problem. What is vital in these tricky situations is to encourage people to engage in "inquiry" into what is happening rather than try to win arguments. One way of doing this is to show the combatants that they can find positive intentions behind the contested behaviour which they themselves would support, were they in that position. To do this they need to pay attention to the context as seen by the other person, or "step into the other's shoes". This helps them become aware of the "multiple realities" that exist and the need for two-way dialogue, rather than debate, to clarify where there is consensus and where the real differences lie.

When the group started to repeat themselves, I stopped the discussion and asked the Chairman to respond first—I wanted to give him the opportunity to create a more positive context for the Chief Executive to speak into. This proved to be a sensible move as, with his political sensitivities, he was able to pick up the lead beautifully and, although pulling no punches, spoke quite eloquently about the range of abilities needed, and how he and the Chief Executive seemed to possess quite complementary skills. This served to improve the atmosphere quite markedly, and when the Chief Executive spoke he was able to handle himself well despite signs that deep down he was probably rather angry. He also took the opportunity to tell his colleagues that he was well aware of his need now to change strategy and style; he had put in motion a number of activities that would help with this task. He also asked his colleagues for help in making the shifts needed. I think many people found this quite surprising from someone who, until this meeting, had seemed as solid and immovable as a wall, and several seemed quite touched.

A conversation is like a journey of discovery—you don't really know what you're getting into until you've made your move and the other person has responded. In other words, the meaning of any conversation is determined not by one's intention but by what follows and the speakers' sense of context (see Chapter 1 on "levels" of meaning). As this process continues, the meaning of the conversation usually becomes clearer as the context itself becomes clearer. But the two are in mutual interaction and therefore it is possible to influence the sense of context, and hence meaning, by what you say next in response to the last remark. Given the criticism the Chief Executive had been subjected to earlier, I felt that it was important that his sense of context be made more positive—i.e. supportive of him—before he responded. His last remarks would have a significant influence on the meaning of the whole event, and I wanted him to be able to deliver these in a good state of mind. The way the Chief Executive responded to the Chairman speaking about complementary abilities indicated that these had had the effect of changing the meaning of the arguments—from a win/lose debate to an exploration of legitimate differences and requisite skills.

By this time, tea was ready to be served, and I asked that people took steps to conclude the discussion over the tea break as the end of the meeting was fast approaching. For this final session, I acted as scribe as the Chairman took over and listed half a dozen action points for them to pick up at the next Board meeting. Everybody then indicated that they had found the event tiring but very helpful, and the Chairman then ended the meeting. We agreed before parting that we would meet a few days later to reflect on the event.

I was pleased that although my original design had turned out to be too complex and time-consuming, the event had gone well and some important learning had come out of the group. They had also been able to sail very close to the emotional wind at times without capsizing, which had been one of the Chairman's initial fears. Little real progress had been achieved at the nitty gritty level of vision statement, strategy, and policy decisions, but most of the group seemed to realize that this was a bridge too far at this stage. I was worried, though, about the "battering" the Chief Executive had taken and how the Chairman was going to manage the next phase of the work.

My working hypothesis, like a conversation, had also been shifted by my experiences over the preceding twelve hours. The group comprised a much wider range of ability, experience, and interests than I had imagined. There were significant differences between the non-executives in their understanding and readiness to work "as a Board" and even greater differences in their relation to the executives, in their grasp of what needed to be done to raise the effectiveness of the Trust. It was clear that they were going to face significant problems in finding a way of working that met their diverse needs and abilities, particularly given their different time commitments to the process. There was a sense that if the tensions between the Chairman and Chief Executive were not managed, the non-executives could become rather peripheral to the process, confining themselves just to "going through the motions" during monthly Board meetings. The event had however identified a number of potential connections between executives and non-executives which, if supported, could improve the level of variety and cohesion and take some of the pressure off the Chairman–Chief Executive relationship.

My final sense of the system I had been working with was that a start had been made but the sense of team identity was very fragile. The contrasting pressures on the executive and non-executive groups were likely to militate against the success of this delicate process unless further "development time" was planned in. Both groups needed to learn to understand and appreciate the beliefs and values of the other, and of the stakeholder groups they represented. The Chairman and Chief Executive would also need to find ways of fashioning a modus operandi that made use of their different interests and skills and of providing an encouraging climate for the development work between the two groups to flourish.

CONCLUSION

This assignment continued for several months longer, involving some sessions with the Chairman, one discussion with the Chairman and the Chief Executive together, and a two-hour session at one of the Board meetings to progress the "vision" statement. Although the awayday had made a useful impact on how the group were relating, relations between the two most senior directors remained problematic. A few months after the last working contact, the Chairman reported that relations, as far as "operational matters" were concerned, were now reasonably effective, but little progress was being made on longer-term "cultural" challenges. He was also bracing himself to make some changes in the non-executive ranks.

Looking back at the event and what followed, I can now see that my main use of systemic and constructionist ideas was in the initial design of the event, working very much from a **first-level cybernetics** (see Glossary) position. This helped me deal with the uncertainties and difficulties that were inherent in the assignment in a more effective way, and this is probably the first thing that consultants new to these ideas should try doing. Although with the systemic approach you may not initially be able to work in the here and now, you can use the ideas to influence how you plan and design your interventions, and so improve the likely connectedness with client concerns; it will also help you develop "contingency thinking" and improve your ability to respond to unexpected shifts and turns during such events.

However, given the way the assignment developed after the awayday, I now feel that I would have been more helpful to my client had I been able to operate more consistently from a second-level cybernetics position. In the next case, in Chapter 4, we move to a description of systemic working from this position. Here again we describe design activity, but in this instance the design is more clearly related to the consultant's here-and-now systemic hypotheses about interaction in the organization, with the consult-ant seeing himself and his views very much as a part of the system.

CHAPTER 4

A work-team consultation

*Giving the client system
time to reframe understandings*

*This case discussion follows from the previous one in several ways. It is
also about a consultation within the public sector, but describes events
that took place over a longer period of time—four months—involving a
range of meetings and interventions. In this case, the participants were
not directors at the "top" of an organization, but middle managers coping
with change in the "engine room" of a complex system. The case illustrates a different way of approaching the problem of the "incompetent
manager". It also demonstrates the way in which the consultant uses
feedback from the on-going process to plan each stage of the work.*

The original need for consultancy in this case arose from a
discussion in the bar at a conference with the Director of
Social Services of one of the new unitary local authorities.
His service had just been incorporated into the Authority, but the
move had brought to the fore a longer-standing issue within their
Social Work Division. The problem had reached the highest levels
within the organization, which made me even more keen to take on
this work and use the project to enhance the reputation of our
partnership.

I used this information to help me understand the meaning of the request for consultation. This is the first step in creating a picture of the context for the work. Knowing that the consultancy would be sanctioned at the highest level in the Authority meant that the work would certainly be supported. I assumed meetings would start on time and the coffee would be hot, but I was also aware that having me there might be seen as the brainchild of the Director of Social Services, and that others in the organization would therefore be less than open and frank with me, fearing what the boss might think. And for my own part, I had to acknowledge that I wanted to do a good job because I have learned that the desire to have a successful outcome can lead me to take a more careful, safe direction in consultancy work and thereby collude with the organization's wish to not "rock the boat".

Some time after the conference, the Director telephoned and gave me the name of the Head of the Social Work Division, Roger. He said that he had put Roger in the picture about us and the discussion we had had. He wanted me to go ahead with the assignment and to regard Roger now as the client. I duly telephoned Roger to make my introduction and to get more information. He began, slightly apologetically, by explaining their budget constraint, and wondering whether I would be able to make a difference with just two or three sessions with the team. He went on to outline the problem.

The Social Work Division contained a Head Office Group, structured to match the main professional functions of their work—Community Work, Juvenile Work, Intermediate Treatment, Health & Mental Services, and the Social Work group itself. This group was co-ordinated by his deputy, Joan. They worked mainly in outlying area offices, and one of these, covering a major conurbation some way from the Head Office, was the focus of the problem. Being distant, the Area team here replicated in its structure the variety of professional disciplines at Head Office—psychologists and legally qualified people as well as social workers. The Head of this Area, named Alan, was qualified in social work. Recently one of the team's psychologists had resigned because she could not work with Alan, and there was also a history of poor relationships between him and the intermediate treatment worker, another psychologist, who was also threatening to leave. Roger was worried because the service was not functioning well in this area, and he feared a problem in recruiting new staff in the present atmosphere.

As the Authority was some way from London, I decided to spend a working day "on the patch", seeing a range of people in different combinations.

My usual practice in beginning consultancy work is to "start at the top". That is, I like to meet the managers who are accountable for the problems in the organization. I do this for several reasons: firstly, I want to meet the managers personally, so that they know who I am and what I'm trying to do. I want to learn about their hopes and fears about the consultancy, and I want to reassure them that I respect the organizational hierarchy. I want to utilize and work within the accountability structure of the organization, and I want also to give this message to everyone in the organization. Although this seems to run counter to the "neutrality" principle, I have found that this "connecting and accepting" behaviour is essential if I am to help everybody who is in any way influencing the problem system to become aware of their active involvement in its maintenance and in its resolution. My role is not to solve the problem, but to perturb the "system" in appropriate ways; only they can solve their problem. I have found through experience that a consultancy is much more likely to run aground if it fails to respect in this way the system's own role in determining the form that changes will ultimately take, once it has been helped to accept the need for changing. This illustrates nicely the concept of **structure-determined change** *(see Glossary), derived from biology.*

The second reason for proceeding in this way is that I am interested to hear how the managers construct the problem. This tells me about their own dilemmas and reflects the values and culture of the organization at the highest levels as well as the resources and support available to them in tackling the problem. This information allows me to make hypotheses about the meaning of the problem for the wider context—i.e. the culture of the new unitary Authority.

With these thoughts in mind, I told Roger I would like to meet him and Joan for an hour first, before going on to a meeting with them and the staff of the Area Office.

THE FIRST VISIT

Roger met me at reception and ushered me through the offices, pointing out different departments and telling me about the new Authority structure. He was enthusiastic and I got a sense of how important it was for him to make his part of this new structure work well. His deputy, Joan, was assigned to manage five area offices, including the "New Town" area. She was quiet during our meeting, deferring to Roger. Together they clarified two specific problems.

One immediate problem was a question of professional quali-fications, which these managers felt unqualified to answer: the intermediate treatment worker, Guy, had gained an additional qualification in family therapy, thinking that it would help in his immediate responsibilities as well as adding to his career pros-pects. However, the Area Manager, Alan, said his qualification was not recognized in local government and he could not allow him to practise his "therapy" in the Area; Guy's view apparently was that he had never been treated with professional respect by Alan. The rest of the staff had polarized around these two protagonists. Joan seemed more bothered by this than was Roger, and they told me the story as though this was an issue where I, as an "expert", could use my professional judgement to decide which view was correct.

This is a very typical challenge to our stance of "neutrality". It would have been very easy to offer an opinion, but I indicated that, while I had personal views, the real answer (more useful to them) to this question would emerge from our further discussions with the staff. I believe consultants can be more helpful to their clients when they show equal interest in all views. This encourages dia-logue, and, from this more open exchange, new ideas and perspectives that can lead the client system to answering its own question are more likely to emerge.

The second, long-standing problem was Alan himself. The man-agers had lost confidence in his ability to create the necessary climate for interdisciplinary work. He seemed to keep a tight con-trol on all the work that was done, and other staff felt constrained and several good people had left the service. This was an issue that exercised Roger.

I also attempted to clarify my role as I saw it at that time. I saw myself offering a consultation that would, hopefully, help people understand what was going on at different levels of the organization; in order to do that, I envisaged meeting the different subgroups and putting the parts together to create a larger picture. I said I would like thirty to forty minutes at the end of the day to share my impressions and do some planning for the future.

Roger and Joan had each clarified what the problems meant to them in their roles within the organization. This began to help me see how different people in the situation were connecting and grouping around the problem, creating a "problem-determined system". I am always concerned when one person is singled-out as being a problem, or the cause of the problem, because it often means it will be a struggle to change this linear view towards seeing the problem as part of a larger, circular and systemic process.

The three of us then set off on the journey to the "New Town" area office, to meet the staff of the unit. When we arrived, we found Alan, his community work and juvenile services specialists, and Guy, the centre of the controversy. The other staff were unable to clear the day on short notice. As we all introduced ourselves I could see everyone was tense and guarded. When I asked what they thought were the problems we needed to address, the discussion quickly degenerated into a series of accusations and defensive replies about the validity of different types of treatments versus professional respect and autonomy. Each person was justifying his or her position, and Alan particularly was citing one official document or government circular after another to support his case. I said we wouldn't get very far unless everyone was able genuinely to understand the position of the others in the group, and I suggested we had a more detailed review of where each of them was "coming from".

It is very difficult to work in a climate of blame and accusation. From a systemic perspective, people are projecting the problem "out there" and not seeing the way in which their own views create a narrow picture that is only a small part of what is going on in the group. This kind of mutual "scapegoating" is a process that isolates parts of the organization; there-

fore, my thought was to do something that would enable people to see more clearly the ways in which they were connected, and how they shared responsibility for the problem as constructed between them.

I went to the flip chart and wrote their names in a circle and began asking each the same questions: "What are your professional connections and reference groups?" "What are the important values you want to hold on to?" "What are the responsibilities you want to carry out in your work, and what personal dilemmas do you experience in doing so?"

This seemed to ease the tension in the group. It became clear, for example, that Guy was primarily interested in career development for himself, whereas Alan was concerned to preserve his authority as the head of an Area going through a period of transition. And it became clear that the Head Office managers felt out of touch with the unit and the way it was being run by Alan.

Hearing this discussion was helpful to me because it planted the seeds for several hypotheses about what was going on. For one thing, I sensed that everyone was lined up against Alan. The area staff were clearly fed up but did not know what to do. I felt it was important not to "join the ranks" and identify Alan as the only problem. Instead, I took the view that another potential problem lay in the gap between the central managers and the Area team, and I explored further the feedback loops between the Area and the managers. For example, Alan did not feel he had a clear mandate about the direction the Area was meant to take, and the staff were not receiving sufficient information about referrers' and clients' feedback about the unit.

Another thought forming in my mind was that the dispute about the validity of Guy's treatment approach had gone on much too long and was probably a red herring for the issue of authority and management support within the Area. I suggested to everyone that often such issues are debated endlessly as a way of testing out who is really in charge and how authority is supported by the larger organization. I then moved the discussion away from the "court-room debate" about who was right and wrong, and onto a process-level discussion about what was necessary for the managers and the Division Head to clarify their position about the way decisions are made concerning the validity and legality of the work carried on in their Areas. This discussion seemed to be helpful. The managers came to realize that because they had avoided contacting the necessary professional bodies they had not been able to decide on a policy about Guy's treatment approach and pass it down to the Area.

Finally, I noticed that Alan became less confident and certain as the meeting wore on. The discussion about management seemed to have the effect of making him more dependent on the managers and more unsure about his own abilities to manage. In fact, at the end of the meeting he came up to me to ask my opinion about a management training course that he was thinking of attending. I wondered whether he wanted some of the management responsibility taken off his shoulders and did not know how to communicate this without losing face or jeopardizing his role in the Division.

Following a tea break, during which I went to a separate room to get into the "observer position" and gather my thoughts, I came back to the group to share my ideas. I wanted to support the hierarchy in the Area and also present a balanced picture of the personal conflict, so I said, "There would inevitably be tension in any unit between new approaches to handling client difficulties and the need to preserve high standards for the sake of the clients. What has happened here is that these positions have been taken up by two people, Guy and Alan, and become polarized. No-one can see a way to resolve it, so others are forced to take sides, or stay out of the debate. The question is, how do the managers want to deal with this inevitable tension, because there will be other occasions in the future when professional conflicts will have to be resolved by management and you need to create a means to do it efficiently." I then added that I would talk separately to Roger and Joan about some ideas that might help them in this task.

The second point I made was that I was aware there was bad feeling about the way they all got along together, and some of the blame for this was being directed at Alan. I certainly did not know the situation well enough after one day to understand all the personalities involved, but I thought these situations became more clear when groups had the opportunity to work together over some time to clarify where they were going, what structures they required, and how work was allocated and to whom. I proposed that they spent some time meeting with Joan for this purpose until I came back to see them in six weeks' time. I was aware of having a limited fee budget for the assignment, and I had been thinking beforehand of ways of creating some sort of network in which on-going work could be done between my visits, and this idea seemed to fit the situation.

Finally, I suggested that all of these problems were taking place in the larger context of the formation of the new Authority, and we did not fully understand all the pressures on those in management positions to change their ways of working. But I wondered if the new emphasis on "market testing" meant some of the human re-sources issues, such as the management style of an Area head, had to take a back seat to management efficiency.

I typically end meetings with some comments of my own (sometimes called an intervention), putting things into a context that acknowledges the client's ideas and feelings but also introduces some new constructs. I hope that these will help the client see the issues in a new light and so offer new choices. In this case, I wanted to highlight the management issues apparent so far, and I wanted to lay the foundation for people to work together to create some joint proposals and strategies. I also wanted to draw everyone's attention to the fact that the problem was greater than just what was happening within that Area office—it involved the future of the Division within the Authority.

Following this meeting, I met again with Roger and Joan. Roger had told me over the telephone he would be able to pay for two or three days' work but we had not finalized these plans, so I was anxious to know what he thought of the day and whether he saw the value in continuing with further meetings. He thought that the day went well because issues were discussed and everyone had a say without the meeting degenerating into a shouting match. I talked about the "management gap" between them and the Area office. I pointed out that often interpersonal problems became ex-acerbated because the Area was isolated and the staff could not see their differences in any wider context than the local context, which simply perpetuated the problems. Roger said, for the first time, that he wanted to begin thinking of other ways in which he could organize that particular Area, and he was aware that he did not fully support the Area Manager. They agreed to the interventions I had made in the previous meeting, and, when Roger left for another meeting, Joan and I devised a plan for her to work with the staff. This was aimed at enabling the group to work together to support Alan's management through weekly meetings, which would produce a mission statement about where the service was going, clarify standards of behaviour for their work, and discuss the structure necessary to implement their plans. She was enthusiastic about taking on this piece of work, although sceptical about whether Alan would actually change.

It seemed to me that Alan and the staff of the Area needed support as a team if they were going to work together. I was also concerned that Alan was not supported very much by management, and, since I would not be able to travel to the Area regularly, it made more sense to connect the management to the Area through Joan's meetings; with any luck, Alan might also find the support to enable him to manage more effectively. Although this intervention might be used by many types of consultants, as a constructionist consultant I was trying to keep in mind that, in the context of change in the Division and the Authority as a whole, some units might be pruned away. It was important therefore to focus on the connection, or lack of it, between the Area and the Head Office management team, and if ultimately the Area had to be re-structured or scrapped altogether, at least the issues would have been faced in a series of development meetings with Joan.

This also illustrates two further ideas we hold. First, because we regard people and their interactions as in continual flux, every action we take or recommend can be viewed as both diagnosis and intervention; so we try to encourage our clients to implement proposals with an inquiring frame of mind. We frame them not as solutions, but as the chance to create experiences for people from which they can go on to learn about their system, and so identify new options. Our proposals allow us to "act", in line with client expectations of consultants, and yet "not act" (in the sense of giving a diagnosis or prescription for change). The latter stance, as we outlined in earlier chapters, leads only to first-order change.

The second idea concerns the pacing of our work with clients. Because it takes time for a system to work through fully the implications of an intervention and begin to understand its meaning, we like to leave several weeks between our visits, as in this instance. We rarely find that things

have evolved as our hypothesis assumed. That provides us with more
information for further productive work, as well as reminding us of our
position in this system as participant observers only.

I then suggested two further sessions as part of my consultancy work. I wanted to meet with the full management team in order to clarify their dilemmas about managing the Area and also in order to devise a strategic plan for the future. I also wanted to include Alan in this process. So I proposed we set up two meetings: one which included the management team and the second which included Alan. For my third visit, I wanted to spend the day with Joan and the staff of the Area to do some team building, which would review the work done by Joan regarding the mission statement and talk over some of the interpersonal problems within the Area.

THE SECOND VISIT

When I arrived for my second visit, I met Roger briefly on his own. Naturally, I was very curious to know what had been happening since the previous visit six weeks earlier. The first thing he reported was that Guy, the intermediate treatment worker at the centre of the storm, had handed in his resignation!

In these situations, people's first expectation is usually to think that
now the "problem" will disappear along with the problem person. But
then they are surprised to find that it pops up again in all sorts of ways
and places. In systemic terms, we see this as showing how the problem has
all along been constituted in the various parts of the system and in the
norms and rules that govern their inter-relationship in that culture. It has
been "projected", for intellectual or political convenience, onto just one or
other individual person. In this instance, Roger had for some time been
worried about the isolation of the Area office and had already been consid-
ering moving it to a new site—so it was not difficult to engage in a more
systemic discussion of the issue with him, and of ways of bringing the area
into a tighter management structure.

Roger brought me into the picture on his sounding about the pros and cons for these proposed changes with a few colleagues.

He also said Joan had been carrying on with the staff meetings at the Area office. These had been going well, but Alan was neither better nor worse in his role as manager.

We moved on to our planned meeting with Roger, Joan, and the heads of the various disciplines in the Head Office team. This included Joan, in her role as manager responsible for the Area offices, and the professionals who monitored the work of the Area staff, together with the Head of the Administration & Management Group, who held the Personnel management brief for the Service. After some discussion about the problem which wandered around without an edge to it, I asked them to describe what would happen if nothing improved over the next three months. This aroused greater concern and brought an urgency to the discussion. Roger decided he would circulate a paper to all managers of the division in order to canvass opinion and pull together some proposals for the future of the "New Town" Area. They were gloomy about Alan's ability to manage the people in the Area, but they agreed it would also be very difficult to dismiss him, because of his professional membership and support from other social work professionals in the Service.

This part of the discussion demonstrates the value of stimulating the tension between holding things as they are and changing things for the future. When people within an organization have identified a problem, they may be reluctant to move forward, but they are also damned if they don't. Using "future questioning" helps people step over immediate blocks and get in touch with another part of their experience, which brings out their energy and suggests new options.

They said they felt there was a dilemma about the professional versus management split in the Service. They could not dismiss Alan because there would be a huge outcry from his fellow professionals, who were unaware of the deep concern about his management skills. Roger, Joan, and the head of Administration & Management decided the best options were:

1. somehow to get him to change; or
2. give him more management support; or

3. re-organize the service in such a way that his failings did not jeopardize the quality of the service or the morale of the staff.

I concluded this first meeting by commenting on the difficulties of moving into the new context of a unitary authority, subject to ideas of "market testing" and "arm's-length" commercial-type contracting. In the old days it was possible to get along with big splits between the professionals and managers, but in the new, more competitive market any inefficiencies might weaken the Authority. So in the current climate the professions have to recognize the role of management, and vice-versa. It was as if this team were hovering between the old and new, wondering if they could challenge the professionals and bring them on board with the managers.

After a break, the head of the social work function had to leave, and Alan joined the group for the second meeting. The idea was that he would come to the second meeting to contribute to a strategic plan for the "New Town" Area, but I had not anticipated the powerful impact this arrangement would have on him. He launched into a speech filled with official documentation jargon to defend his position and the future of the Area's services. I quickly became aware of how vulnerable he felt, and I tried to think of a way to acknowledge this but also share the vulnerability amongst the whole group. I interrupted Alan, saying there had been problems in the Area for many and complicated reasons but we were not here to put anyone on trial; rather the Service was being reviewed in terms of the work it does for the community and the most efficient management structure to carry out its tasks; our job was to outline what needed to be done to answer all the questions about the future of the Service.

As a consultant, I inevitably make mistakes, particularly working on my own, and miss important points which, with hindsight, seemed to be staring me in the face. All we can do is take the time, during or after the consultation, to reflect on the meaning for us and the organization of missing the point, and be flexible enough to change our thinking and our techniques to fit the new understanding. In systemic terms we try to think of the experience as feedback about ourselves in interaction with the organization, rather than personal "error".

I then talked about the anxiety and uncertainty they must feel about being a part of a service that was not working well. "Would somebody be blamed?" "Would drastic changes have to be made?" "Would people be redeployed, or would the Area close altogether?" This reframing of the context of the discussion helped the group adopt a more sympathetic attitude towards Alan and changed the way they thought about the purpose of the meeting.

Next I asked them individually to write down the three most important things they thought must be done to clarify the future of the Service from their own perspective in the organization. I put their ideas on a flip chart and combined them into five areas that needed further clarification. We then went through each of the five to decide (a) which actions would be taken by whom and (b) by what deadline.

This work is an example of moving from the meaning level to the action level. At a certain point in this discussion, the group seemed to reach some sort of consensus about the situation and the fact that something had to be done. At this juncture, it is essential to ask a group to commit themselves to some action on the basis of this meaning. These actions we know will change the context and then lead naturally to further new actions.

The five areas were:

1. Internal relations had to be addressed. Joan agreed to continue offering meetings to set out standards of practice and a scheme for auditing work. She agreed to offer team-building meetings to the staff.

2. There was a need for client feedback about the Area in the form of a questionnaire to clients and referrers.

3. There was a need for stronger links between management and the Service through more contact with Joan.

4. Thinking needed to begin about the role of the "New Town" Area in the long-term development of the Service.

5. Interdisciplinary relationships needed to improve, and so Roger and Joan were going to consult the various professional representatives about drafting some new, attractive job descriptions to use when recruiting staff to replace those who had left.

During my de-briefing session with Roger and Joan at the end of the day, I was surprised to see how keen Joan had become in the whole process. She was animated and enthusiastic. They both appreciated that we had produced clear guidelines and action paragraphs, but Joan said she had learned during the day about the management needs for such a Service, and the limitations that some professional staff have about managing.

I certainly had no clear idea of what the outcome of the meeting might be when I began the day. It was clear, however, that the management team had appreciated the opportunity to carry out management tasks and begin the process of change, but on whose terms?

I wondered whether the writing was appearing on the wall and whether management solutions would prevail over further attempts to lift Alan up to the task. I felt a few regrets about this—for example, I wondered if I should have done some team-building work in the Area earlier. But I also felt that the group, including Alan, was moving in the direction of solving their problem, and I had the impression that even Alan would feel some relief at not being pressured to manage beyond his ability.

THE THIRD VISIT

My third visit took place about three months after the first and had been planned as a review of Joan's on-going work and a team-building session with the staff of the Area. When I arrived at the Area office, I was greeted by Alan, who seemed like a different person on his own turf. The building was not very conducive to a good team atmosphere. It was a grand Victorian building with high-ceilinged rooms, which were closed off to the central corridors with heavy fire doors.

My aim during the day was to provide a safe forum for discussion of their issues, to organize some exercises or "structured discussions", and to share my own views of what I thought was going on. When our meeting started I was introduced to the staff present, including Joan from Head Office. Meeting the staff group as a whole for the first time, I was most curious to know how they were dealing with the insecurity about their future. Although I was expecting strong feelings of anger or vulnerability, it turned out that they had recently learned that one of their client "purchasers" had decided to use another source for part of their requirements, and as a result they felt things really had to change.

I asked about the relations between Alan and the staff group which had been an original source of concern. They had worked on this during their Friday meetings with Joan, and several had agreed that they still had communication problems and difficulties in trusting each other. They were critical of Alan for being over-controlling, but things had got somewhat better. The Community Work specialist did not join in the criticism of Alan, but *everyone* felt some responsibility for the lack of trust amongst them. One person said that people seemed very guarded and another added that they didn't seem to really respect each other's work.

When I hear such comments, I often construct a hypothesis about interdisciplinary rivalries and a very uncertain loyalty of the individuals to their unit. When I shared this thought, several people agreed that they could not give their full loyalty to this Area because it either was not secure enough or they were being pulled in opposite directions towards their own disciplines. I then turned to Joan and said, "It sounds like it may be hard for them to work together unless they feel secure—and that's a job for management". Joan agreed that the Area had seemed to her like a battleground where disciplines vied for power, and she was trying to help them feel more connected to management by seeing more of her. We also talked at length about the divided loyalties each one felt between discipline and Area.

I try to move from discussions of pertinent issues to exercises (from meaning to action) that allow participants to try out new ways of relating to each other. In systemic terms, I am creating a new feedback loop between two or more people, which may create new patterns of behaviour in the unit. In this case, I was thinking that some experience of working together and acknowledging their own doubts and limitations with each other might bind them together a bit more.

I asked them to present briefly a case they had worked on collaboratively with another worker and to discuss a bit that went well, a bit that did not and something they had learned from their colleague. As the group carried out this exercise, it did not seem to be a new or challenging experience for them, so I assumed that it was not addressing the heart of the matter. I wondered if perhaps the pairing format and the focus on "working together" was too indirect a way into the real issue for the group—the lack of professional respect from others. So when the group came together, I suggested they share what they feel goes on in the Area which makes people feel that there is a lack of mutual professional respect. This turned into a lively, heated discussion, including many small details of the working day, and certainly cleared the air for the staff group.

I had wanted to spend some time alone with Alan, so I could give him some feedback and the opportunity to talk to me privately if he wished. In view of this, I had arranged beforehand to have lunch alone with him on this day. I told him why I had set this time aside for the two of us, but after a few minutes it was clear that he was not going to let down his guard, nor did I want to push him in any direction he did not want to go. I asked if these had been hard times for him, and he replied that they hadn't particularly and that it was all part of the job of being in charge of an Area. I gave him some feedback about what others thought of his management style—that is, talking too much, not listening, and leaving people feeling crushed or unappreciated in the wake of his own standards and procedures. I remarked on the dilemma of running the Area according to *his* standards versus drawing other people out and creating standards of practice through a consensual process. He held his opinion in favour of his own standards, but he did also say he was still looking for ways to get further management training. "That is, if they still want me after they reorganize the Service", he added, jokingly. We then talked about how difficult it must be to be asked to do things beyond his own level of experience.

My relationship with Alan left me feeling frustrated, and I wondered if this was a sign that I was in danger of seeing the issue too much from management's perspective. (This is a useful indicator of a loss of neutrality and a signal to check one's current perspective and state of curiosity.) I also wondered if he was telling me that he really believed he was the wrong man in the wrong place. During my work with the Service, I had been in contact with him through several letters, and I had discussed the possibility of further management training, but I was disappointed that I could

not have set up a series of role consultations with him. This would have
allowed our relationship to develop, and for him to use me to develop a
more systemic understanding of the situation and the dilemma he was
facing. This is one of the tribulations faced by the systemic worker: on the
one hand, the depth of the approach helps you become more aware of the
wide variety of emerging issues; on the other, the focus on priorities
ensures that you have to turn away from most!

After lunch I thought it was important to continue working on
the theme of trust by setting up an exercise that might suggest a
more open model of communication amongst staff members which
is so crucial in organizations where teams serve clients. I asked
them to join in pairs and talk together for ten minutes about what
their partner did that was helpful to them. Following this exercise, I
began to draw the day to a close. I gathered on a flip chart the
things they had learned or understood about the organization during the day, and from this I asked them to consider ways these
points could be supported by changing the structures and operating procedures in the Area. This led to an active planning session in
which the group reorganized the timing and agendas for various
staff meetings—for example, some were to be attended by Joan,
some were to focus on case discussions, and others were to focus
on a review of how they were working together.

In the car park at the end of the day I was speaking alone to
Joan. She felt the day had been supportive for the Area staff as well
as Alan, but she was pessimistic about Alan changing his management style. She would wait to see whether the new structures made
a significant difference, but she also reminded me that she could
not continue to put the same amount of time into supporting the
Area as she had in the past few months. We agreed a date for a
follow-up meeting with Roger in a few months' time and I said
good-bye.

A week before the follow-up meeting, I received a phone call
from Joan, who said that the Management Team had recently made
the decision to move the Area office to a new location, according
to a plan similar to the one discussed at our second meeting. The
Area would be managed more closely from Head Office, and most
of the management responsibilities would thus be taken from

Alan's shoulders. She said for the time being there was no need for a follow-up meeting but they might need some help later on to re-design the "New Town" Area and integrate it more with the pattern of other area offices.

CONCLUSION

Looking back on this piece of work, it seems as though Roger and his Management Team had gone some way down the road of changing the Area's management structure before calling in a consultant. Perhaps in the back of their minds they hoped for a miracle—the transformation of Alan's style—or they wanted a final confirmation that they were making the right decision. There were no miracles, but I felt by being there and opening up the issue of management in the Area, it allowed everyone—managers, Alan, and staff—to express themselves and to address the various possibilities for change. It also brought home to me the implication of the systemic view that organizations never cease changing. There is never the possibility of a "clean" ending to a systemic consultation. As a consultant, you cannot help forming your next hypothesis, being interested in the linkages you now see, but then you have to turn away and allow the client to apply their learning from the effects you *were* able to have on their system.

In this case, I was left with the feeling that there was an invisible barrier that prevented much exploration of the Service and Roger's relationship with senior management and the Authority. But many consultations are like that, and there is always work to be done with those working beneath the barrier. In fact among the consequences of the work were:

- the Management Group working together to produce some strategic plans;
- Joan's increasing confidence at working at the interface between managers and professionals;
- Alan's opportunity to put his case forward publicly while simultaneously acknowledging his limitations as a manager;
- the Area staff having the opportunity to voice their frustrations and build some new working relationships.

In the next chapter, we look at a case where the consultant was in a position not only to work with the top manager (as in Chapter 3), but also with the *whole* organization, rather than just a part, as in this case. It also points up another aspect of this case—how does an organization manage and control innovation in a context of devolved authority? The danger, as with the Area Office Manager, is that useful innovation gets too easily snuffed out when its threatening implications for stability and personal security are not countered by clear corporate-level encouragement of innovation, and guidance about its desired direction. In the next case, innovation was clearly signalled and enacted by the leader, and the problem was more about releasing inhibitions to innovation at all levels of the organization.

CHAPTER 5

A whole-organization consultation

Widening the conversations about change

In this chapter, we look at how systemic principles can be applied when working with a typical successful private-sector company. In contrast to Chapters 3 and 4, where we worked with the leadership group and a middle-management group, we show here the advantage gained by engaging, literally, the "whole system" in different types of conversations about change. This case also shows how the constructionist frame of working can help people make the shift from seeing problems in certain people to seeing the problem in the system of beliefs and the connected meanings that everybody makes from their interactions. This shift enables people to begin to explore different options for tackling issues.

Another concept illustrated in this case is the way in which a problem emerges as people communicate about distinctions they believe are relevant to good performance. Talking together, they come to agree that they are seeing the same thing as "problematic".

As we indicated in Chapter 1, feedback loops act to establish a context in which certain behaviour comes to mean "problem" to other members of a system. However, their response towards the identified "problem person" tends to reinforce the behaviour that they are seeing as problematic.

In our work, we try to establish an important pre-condition for communication—a belief in others' relevant experience and a shared basis of experience and vocabulary; and then we try, primarily, to allow people to experience many different types of communication about a diverse range of issues. We now call this process "widening the conversation".

What does a leader do when the organization is busy, performing well and profitably, and yet seems to contain tensions, inefficiencies, and splits? How does one even start to have a conversation within the organization about what one sees as unsatisfactory without raising the expectation of change, so that all the reactions to threatened change start to appear, without even the benefit of a clear and shared vision of the change that people want? The dilemma is about protecting today's performance by not trying to fix what plainly "ain't broke" and yet perhaps risking tomorrow's performance by not trying to improve what is less than satisfactory now.

These were some of the issues that the Head of a sales organization in the electronics industry believed he was facing. This unit was part of a successful European multi-national, involved in a rapidly growing segment of the market, the design of new applications for micro-circuits in the products of other industries. The organization was 70 strong in the United Kingdom. It was organized as a flat structure, with separate functions for product marketing, design and development, applications sales, sales administration, as well as finance and business development. A distinction was made between direct sales to clients and those made through a distribution network of smaller organizations structured to match the functions of the sales company.

The leader of the sales company, Gordon, was designated General Manager. Some time previously, he had been invited to attend a training event, arranged by the Group Personnel department for junior management from across Europe, at which we had introduced the ideas of participative work design through the medium of a workplace simulation. Gordon had been impressed by the level of insight and positive contribution that seemed to be triggered by this simulation. What, he asked, could we do that might help him to get his people more actively involved in developing their organization?

TALKING ABOUT THE DESIGN OF AN INTERVENTION

As we prepared to follow-up Gordon's invitation to "put a proposal in writing for discussion", a preliminary hypothesis guided us. Gordon had not asked Personnel to do this work. Did he want to maintain a position of strong leadership? He was certainly very intense and bottom-line-orientated and seemed ambitious. Was being innovative an important belief? Or did he think the issues he wanted to tackle were not responding to more conventional approaches? Was this why the participative approach had grabbed his interest? This suggested a leader who, perhaps as a chosen style or perhaps reflecting perceived limits to his authority, felt constrained in what he could ask his people to support. Perhaps a sensitivity about the extent of his influence was why he did not feel he wanted to delegate this idea to Personnel.

We wrote to Gordon, inviting him to meet with us first by himself, but then to involve a small group of others in thinking how a simulation could be embedded in some sort of event that met the needs of the organization as seen by and agreed by this wider subgroup. The first meeting actually involved Gordon and his Planning Manager, Arthur. They quizzed us about the content of the simulation. We had suggested one designed for "knowledge workers" (see Figure 4). It challenges teams to design, market, and build a tower block to a negotiated price, meeting customer requirements on specification and timescale. We got a distinct impression that Gordon was committed, acting as sponsor of our ideas. Again, we had the sense of someone leading this organization from the front, but slightly concerned he might be getting too far ahead. This was confirmed as we asked how our ideas for a workshop event fitted with recent organization development interventions.

We quickly learned that "team" was a significant word for this group. The top management group, some eleven people, had recently undergone several "team-development" experiences, mostly focusing on trust-building, openness, and communication styles. They were now trying to extend "teaming" to the rest of the

The simulation is divided into two stages. The first sets up a traditional organization, with functional and site separation. There is a customer, who must be negotiated with, and a production unit which must implement what is agreed with the customer, meeting competitor prices as well as the customer's service needs. The experience of meeting these requirements in a traditional setting is analysed by the participants before they are guided through a process for re-designing the work-system. They then have the chance to experience meeting new customer needs in this different work setting, which they have designed. The performance comparison between the two work settings can be discussed, sharpened by the data about costs, time, and customer satisfaction collected during the two production runs.

The simulation helps introduce a systemic way of thinking. Within the day, participants switch perspectives several times: from an unfamiliar role in a traditional organization structure to an internal consultant critiquing the interaction of the system; from change agent to participant worker operating in their own redesigned system, and finally to the consultant critiquing role again. Switching roles in this way, and taking on unfamiliar roles, helps people get in touch with the inter-connectedness of behaviour in organizations. They also understand how the context set by organization structure and systems affects the meaning people make of their experiences. They can see how problem behaviour can also be understood as people trying to make roles work as they believe was intended. In the critique of the simulated organization's performance, people experience the effectiveness of looking at the whole system, and of considering how behaviour in one part of the system produces effects elsewhere that in the end connect with the starting behaviour. Context and meaning, meaning and behaviour, actions and relationships are all seen as interconnected.

Figure 4. **Simulating an organization**

organization. However, there were counter-pressures, a sense of "them" versus "us" building up. The senior management group thought that "team" represented a threat to some of the other people who wanted to be "entrepreneurs" in their work style. To us, there seemed to be some connection to other problems—the competition between functions over "grey areas", perhaps including the boundary with the production side of the business. Arthur told us that since the first teaming event for the wider organization, three groups had been working for months on the issues that had surfaced: communication, design monitoring, and organization and management systems. Progress had been disappointing on all three, and the latter group had effectively copped out of the work altogether.

A week later, as agreed, we met the whole senior management "team" for a wider discussion about what development might be appropriate for the organization. Despite their teaming work, this group came across to us as highly competitive amongst themselves, and diverse in culture and work styles. They ranged from the representative of a predominantly female department to a male, technical, expert, and linear-thinking group, who were, to say the least, "robust" in their feedback.

Their response to us was guarded. As well as reflecting their earlier "team development" experience, this also seemed to be a statement about how training was handled in the company, as something that was "done" to people rather than being something people chose to meet their need. All were agreed, however, that the organization had problems; the open talk of "them" and "us" was felt to stand in the way of greater involvement by people in the business operations essential for customer service, but also for the ability of the operation to cope with increasing activity levels.

At this point we felt strongly the need to help this group differentiate the approach we were proposing from their previous experience of organization development events. We thought we were being seen as just another pair of outsiders who were going to make them fit some prescription we had for "good" organizational behaviour. What we had to communicate through our interaction with the group over the next hour or so was our confidence in a process by which they would be able to discover their own solutions to issues that they owned.

We decided to help the group work out the criteria for a development event that would be successful, helping the organization to work differently and more effectively. We asked the group to brainstorm ideas, and then reduced these to a manageable list of requirements against which they would be able to review what our involvement had helped them achieve. The final list read as follows:

- key issues identified and owned by all;
- teams volunteering to tackle these;
- communication achieved and accepted, so that "them/us" feelings were no longer relevant;
- comfort and trust evident in dealings between people across the organization;
- greater understanding of differences and their link to certain roles.

The process seemed to achieve its objective, and we left "onside" with this group for the moment.

ESTABLISHING THE DIFFERENCE— USING THE PROPOSAL TO START THE CHANGE PROCESS

By this point, we had broadly agreed with Gordon on the shape of some interactions, which he would be able to have with the rest of the organization in the coming months, that would address his dilemma about taking action and yet would also meet the concerns voiced at least by his senior management team. There were two tasks now. The first was to enable Gordon to show that the consultation process with the senior management group had influenced the proposal he was to take to them. The second was to work on how Gordon would communicate the proposals to the rest of the organization, so that the intervention would be seen as clearly different from their earlier experience.

One hypothesis we used was that the process by which teaming had been introduced, involving the senior management group first, and subsequently introducing the idea of teams to the rest of the organization, was itself linked to the issue of "them" and "us". We thought that it would help to undermine such beliefs if the whole organization now had the same experience, with senior management being "diluted" in the rest of the organization.

We also wanted to be seen to address the feelings about training expressed by the senior managers at our meeting. It was important to use different language about the process that Gordon now wished to set rolling. We proposed to frame his initiative as "organization development" and to stress that although there might be some learning in the process, it was more about people teaching themselves how to increase their effectiveness in their roles within this business.

Gordon would talk of his initiative as "exploring how to handle the development of people, careers, and service in a flat organization setting". The concern with communication would be addressed by introducing the concept of an organizational "conversation", emphasizing the importance of bringing together people who did not normally exchange their views, as well as finding new means for communicating at different levels from those that were the convention within the company. We proposed to set the simulation within a wider workshop event, which would be presented as an opportunity for interaction and sharing views about the future. This workshop itself would be set within an on-going process of organization development work by project teams that would emerge from the planned intervention.

The shape of the intervention that had emerged from our consultations could now be established in a proposal. There would be three Workshops in all, to include every member of staff, managers, receptionists, and security. Senior management were scattered randomly across the three Workshops. We planned to hold all three within a month, so that everyone in the organization would very quickly all have had the same experience. There would be a follow-up event for the whole organization later, to integrate the conclusions of each of the separate groups. From that later event, the whole group would decide what should be the focus of work to develop the organization and overcome any difficulties they had agreed were important.

Each event would start with the group assembling at 16:00 at a local conference centre, where they would be resident for the two nights. The first session before dinner on the first evening was designed to focus specifically on the workshop's purpose and structure, drawing as appropriate on background information, such as that obtained from the staff survey. The following day was devoted to the simulation and its evaluation. On the third day, until lunch, the group would have the opportunity to identify and reflect on the learnings from the simulation, and to discuss their application back in the organization. Within this design, we planned to focus on the way problems are created at a number of levels, with each level represented by a different kind of communication. The introduction of communication at different levels of organizational experience is what we have called "widening the conversation".

WIDENING THE CONVERSATION: I—
AT THE LEVEL OF CORPORATE MYTH

The first level of widening was designed to make people more aware of the different levels of context that influence the meaning they draw from the actions of others in reaction to their own behaviour. As explained in Chapter 1, episodes can shift their meaning when viewed in relation to corporate culture rather than at the usual level of inter-role relationship. What might seem insubordinate between a director and a clerk, as their roles prescribe their relative authority, could be seen as fully responsible, for example, in the context of a corporate culture that valued unscreened feedback from the "front line".

Gordon's introduction to the first Workshop group produced a story that we had not heard before. It represented a "myth" from the corporate culture of the bigger Group, and its use proved very fruitful. Gordon recalled a chief executive who had been part of a strategic review meeting held by the President of the whole Group and all his operating company leaders. Asked about the state of the business as they saw it, this chief executive was appalled to hear one after another of his peers painting a rosy picture. The pressure to conform was huge, but this individual stood his ground and told it the way he saw it, about frustrated customers doing the firm's quality control job for it. He was ushered out to meet the President alone, everyone else assuming he was being shown the best window to jump from. In fact, he was being listened to, chapter and verse, because it was clear to the President that anyone who risked so much had to have something important to say.

We used this story in the first and last sessions of each Workshop, to challenge participants to fit the culture and "speak the undiscussable". We urged people to think of episodes in which the behaviour of others had reflected this corporate myth. The event design reinforced this story and produced a clear shift in the level of "unspeakability" achieved by each group between their first and last sessions. It represented the first way in which the conversation was widened by the intervention design.

WIDENING THE CONVERSATION: II— AT THE LEVEL OF "ANALOGIC" COMMUNICATION, USING SPACE AND POSITION

We also wanted to widen the range of language that people felt able to use. We know that when the state of relationships is an issue, whether between couples or within an organization, people seem to fight shy of talking plainly and communicate more by "acting out" their feelings; this is called **analogic** *(see Glossary) communication, as opposed to verbal communication, which is called "digital". In one sense, this results in a net loss, as analogic language is typically more difficult to interpret although it possesses the power to clarify important realities.*

We asked the whole group to stand in a line, with those who felt most empowered in their work standing on the left, and those who felt least empowered on the right. They could adjust their position by looking at where others stood and challenging them to explain "why there and not here". In effect, we were giving people this opportunity to make a statement without saying anything. And, of course, for everyone (but particularly the senior management group), there was the chance to see where others stood and to begin the conversation "Why do they put themselves there?"

On the final day of the Workshop, we again used space as a means of expression. We asked people to go and stand in relation to others so that they expressed how connected or remote they felt from the others in their work situation. This sorting process took usually less than five minutes, the degree of laughter and noise indicating that people realized they were making statements that in words would be very risky. They were asked to question others if they felt that their position was inappropriate. We quickly captured on flip charts the system map thus created, while asking each obvious subsystem to think of how they would characterize themselves in a single word, which we recorded against their place on the map. In their separate subsystems we then asked them to explain the degree of closeness/separateness they felt to the other subsystems—why the system map looked this way. Finally, they had the chance to voice observations prompted by their feelings at finding themselves in their particular place on the system map. A few brave souls made some forceful comments at this point, comments that we do not believe would have been heard through any of the more conventional processes. "I feel on the outside", said one whose role involved liaising with the production centres in Europe. "And yet I know that I should be right in there, in the middle. But I can't get in there. I don't feel that people give a damn in reality about the working relations with our plants."

WIDENING THE CONVERSATION: III— AT THE LEVEL OF PARTICIPATION

Normally, whatever senior management's desire to involve their people more in key decisions, one factor gets in the way. For people to communicate, there has to be a necessary minimum of shared experience, and a sense of equal relevance of the experience held by each side. In normal situations, people specialize in their work. That represents one level of inhibition to developing understanding through communicating. Then there is the separate specialization by hierarchy, with certain subject matter, policy, and strategy, for instance, held to be suited only for handling by a select group, seeded through their length of service and past levels of performance. Each of these specialist groups develops its own sub-language and shares particular types of experience, different from the rest of the organization, in everyday conversations. It is very difficult for "outsiders" to share verbally with the "insiders" from their separate experience base and feel themselves making any impact on the beliefs and ideas of the "insiders".

The beauty of the simulation of a fictitious operation is that it levels people and gives everyone a common experience base from which to join in communicating. If normal roles can be substituted as well—the secretary becoming the MD and the MD a construction-site worker, with the finance controller becoming the customer—then people begin to get a priceless chance to gain experience from a different perspective within a typical organization. Now everyone has a basis in experience from which to communicate on the level about what makes an organization work. Add to this the experience of being involved in redesigning a workplace, and people begin to feel empowered. This occurs, we believe, because people are experiencing themselves as effective. They risk making a contribution, because it is safe and distant from their everyday role, but they find that what they say is recognized as valid and used by the group.

What happened with this client was that people began making observations to the consultants and to each other about how the simulation experience mirrored what they saw happening at work. For example, two of the senior managers sat together as "The Customer" during the first stage of one simulation, with no-one talking to them but obviously hectically busy making plans that affected The Customer. "Why don't they come and ask us?", said one in exasperation. "We could tell them things that would save one hell of a lot of wasted effort. I know they're heading up a blind alley." And then he added: "It gives me a creepy feeling. I think this is what our customers probably feel like too often." Later on, as the time pressure mounted, and still the design was not finalized and costed and negotiations with the customer were stalled as a result, a sales engineer produced a ripple of embarrassed laughter as he exclaimed: "This is just like us. We get so in love with the design process that we forget time, and the competition. Then we have to panic and do something heroic to pull it back from the brink. There has to be a better way!"

WIDENING THE CONVERSATION: IV— AT THE LEVEL OF RELATIONSHIP

This particular intervention resulted from our systemic hypothesis about the meaning of the behaviour that people were finding to be problematic. If "teaming" was such a difficulty in this organization across a perceived "them and us" divide, did it reflect that people had not had the experience of conversation, as distinct from the normal "telling" that people think of as conversation (particularly in male-dominated and internally competitive organizations)? Our intention was therefore to set up an experience that would enable people to listen and hear each other at a different level from the normal, and to enable this to happen between people who did not normally get to relate in this way.

On the final day we facilitated the working of each subgroup, reintroducing some of the ideas that were provided as a starter to the redesign process during the simulation. For example, one group were concerned at the "gap" they perceived between their unit, which handled customer orders of items in high demand, and the factories located in other countries, supposedly servicing "global" demand. Could they trust the information they were given by these nationally located production units, or were the latter always giving priority to their "local" sales company?

Next, the other subgroups, in sequence, were asked to think of how this behaviour of the system served some positive purpose. At some points, we asked whether there was a "voice" from some missing subsystem that needed to be heard. In the case of the "global"-factory/"local"-sales-company issue, this focused attention on the potential contribution of the liaison unit that earlier had voiced its frustration at not being taken seriously by the "core" of the sales company, feeling "shut out" from the degree of integration that they wanted.

After a few rounds, we asked the groups to identify what they thought would be lost, and by whom, if the behaviour underlying the issue were stopped or altered. An example that surfaced in the case of the factory/sales company issue was an awareness that the sales company might relax and take less care in forecasting their requirements and in keeping close to the customer to get the earliest possible intimation of future requirements.

This exercise had a marked effect. In part we believe this results from the instruction that the problem-holding subgroup should listen and not counter the ideas coming from the others. In part this is made easier by the second experience of difference contained in the process—the experience of hearing others think of the positive aspects of the problem behaviour for the wider system and the losses involved in changing it.

After each subsystem had had a chance to experience this method of "inquiry" and "peer-consultation", we moved on to the identified "teaming" issues. The same process was followed, but this time each subgroup offered to the "problem-holding" subgroup their impressions of:

- what that subgroup did well and gained as a team;
- what and who would lose if the subgroup were to become more effective as a team.

Each team recorded the gains and losses as these surfaced from the contributions of their peers.

Once this cycle of work had been completed, each subgroup discussed together:

- what they would need from other subsystems in order to play their part in changing the problem behaviours;
- what they might offer others to enable them to provide what this subsystem needed in order to achieve the changes they had identified.

This activity led naturally into two subsequent parallel activities. First, each subsystem appointed "plenipotentiaries" to begin a process of negotiating with the other subsystems for the changes they needed in return for the changes they could offer. They reported back at intervals to their colleagues. In the meantime the latter were busy drafting a statement of their intent in changing, in the form of a series of "provocative propositions". These are very general statements about how a unit wishes to work with their internal and external customers on their part of the organizational task. This approach is intended to steer people away from thinking about problem solving and the focus on what doesn't work. This activity helps people appreciate how "leadership" can be practised by people at all levels in an organization. A simple example of such a proposition would be: "in this department, each individual will take personal responsibility for sharing knowledge and expertise with each other person and with people from other units". These propositions were to guide the continuing work of the subsystems after the Workshop, and to provide a focus for evaluating the feedback produced by the negotiators.

In effect, these activities were designed to enhance participants' awareness of a systemic way of thinking about relationships—how there is more than one way of explaining or looking at a situation, and hence more than one way of acting quite sincerely with the organization's interests at heart, even when others experience this action as problematic and unhelpful. This alternative way of thinking, experienced in this issue–dis-solving process that we had taken the group through, would, we believed, reinforce the impact of the simulation and the learnings from it. The final plenary worked on achieving this integration and then building commitment to continue the work outside the Workshop setting.

LEARNINGS

The effect of involving the complete system in discussions and problem solving was high on most people's learning lists. They could see how communication was made more effective when everybody could be involved in talking about problems. They could see how feedback was obtained in this process and the benefits this had. However, they could also see the importance of using a level of listening different to that which they normally used and were aware of the effect on performance when this was not done. They became aware of how their own presuppositions "screened out" information, and how the hierarchical context and role ideas also led to people not being heard when in fact they had valuable insights to offer. Interestingly, the groups also began to see the need for a proactive approach to perceived barriers in organizations, having experienced in the simulation how the safety of the "game" had enabled some to challenge the system, with beneficial results for themselves and the task. Taking responsibility and getting involved were other ways in which this stance was recognized.

All this and the effects of the widening of the conversation about the organization issues had clearly moved the organization on in the way that Gordon had wanted. This was the point at which we felt we could leave the assignment, knowing that the system was already behaving in a different way, and that its people had a platform of shared experiences from which they could continue their wider dialogue, reinforcing their learning about a different way of developing their organization.

SEPARATING FOR CLIENT SELF-DEVELOPMENT

We decided to write to Gordon offering some alternative ways of viewing the original examples of disempowered behaviours that senior management had pointed out to us: subordinates "whinge-ing"; people not speaking out; people pushing responsibility back to senior management, etc. These were not our answers, and are very different from the normal "final recommendations" of a con-sultancy intervention. We were presenting our systemic hypothesis about the interconnection of behaviours around the problem in a form that we hoped would stimulate the client's own ability to find a solution. By being so unusual, but connected to the prob-lem's dis-solution, in presenting our ideas, there is a strong probability that in future problem situations, the client's people will use the same route to finding further solutions. This is our route to the learning organization. The dilemmas we proposed were as follows:

- If you are a manager and have a particular view of what behav-iour leads to success, for yourself and the company, you may feel that anyone else who does not behave as you do is missing out on the possibility of also being successful, and so needs "encouraging" in the same way that you remember yourself being "encouraged". However, this is what others may experi-ence as being pushed, delegated to, "teamed", and otherwise treated as someone without power.

- If some people with authority exhibit "leadership" behaviour, and if the Company is seen to support their special role with "leadership" training, then others may feel it is disruptive and harmful to the organization for them *not* to show appropriate "followership" behaviour. However, they then show what others may see as behaviour that blocks delegation and refuses responsibility, etc.

- If a few people in a senior position in an organization take special pains to improve their team-working, then others may feel they must not be challenged. So they may act less competently than they are, so that the managers can demonstrate their superior competence.

- If management people talk about "right" decisions, and if their behaviour at meetings confirms this, then people who see an additional aspect of an issue, without being certain they have the "right" answer, will tend to hold their counsel, because they cannot provide what the culture values.

- If it is very important to the company to achieve operational goals, and time is fully utilized, then people may feel it irresponsible to undertake additional tasks, knowing that there is not the time available to carry them and their existing tasks through; however, others may see this as "pushing responsibility back up to the top", refusing to act in an empowered way.

- If other people's remuneration depends on the achievement of goals to which you contribute, then you might feel that it is not collegial behaviour to undertake additional responsibilities that can only be met at the expense of those other goals. However, others may see this as refusing to be a good member of the larger team, helping the whole organization to meet its objectives.

This final intervention reflects our belief that organizations change more effectively at the level of their culture and behavioural norms if problems are approached from the assumption of positive motivation, rather than by "blaming" and negative labelling. People tend not to be deliberately obstructive, and the appearance of this is more probably because they are just stuck. The key to dis-solving such cultural problems lies, we believe, in widening in many ways the conversation within the organization about its development.

CONCLUSION

In this assignment, we tried to provide the whole combination of ingredients that Keeney (1983) proposes any "problematic system" requires. First there is the need for "a sufficient range of sensors to detect difference". Next, the system needs "a sufficient range of varied behaviour to facilitate the creation of difference". Finally, the system has to be able to link these two ingredients, to create self-corrective feedback. Our process for developing the intervention design with the client, as well as the first and second conversation-widening processes referred to above, had all worked to develop our client's sensors of difference. The simulation and the shift to the corporate myth level of context, as well as the total participative structure of the events, were all meant to draw out new behaviours from which the system would evolve new patterns of relationship less problematic than the current ones. The final corrective component we provided in the fourth conversation-widening process—by modelling the application of systemic thinking, which privileges connections and positive explanation over competitive differentiation and blaming. By providing these "sensors of difference", "sources of new behaviour", and "recursive linkages between them", we believe we facilitated the development of a self-corrective organizational system.

* * *

This and the two previous chapters have presented just three cases from a wide range of our experience of working systemically in organizations. Some of the ways in which we have operationalized the concepts presented in Chapter 1 can be seen in these case studies. In the chapters that now follow, especially Chapter 6, we provide a more comprehensive view of the extent of our progress, as well as the path we took to reach our present position. In particular, we try to show the links between the task of getting work, of doing it, and of becoming a constructionist consultant.

PART III

METHODOLOGY— DEVELOPING CONSTRUCTIONIST CAPABILITIES

"All descriptions . . . are a creation. We do not live in a universe but in a multiverse with as many descriptions as there are willing describers. Beauty is agreed upon consensually through social interactions, conversations. Things are what we agree to call them."

Paul Watzlawick

CHAPTER 6

The methodology so far . . .

Work in progress

At some stage in a journey of exploration like this, it becomes possible to step back and "punctuate" one's experience, to move, in our case, from the level of philosophical quest to that of methodology—the practical applications of the principles and ideas that underpin the systemic and constructionist perspective. Because of the differences between the originating context and the context of application, this could never be a straightforward translation of principles and methods. We need to identify the new principles and position (what Bernstein, 1983, calls the "beyond" position) that would support creative conversations between the two contexts. In Chapter 2 we identified ten of these principles, and in this chapter we review some of the consequences for consulting practice. We also look at a number of practical approaches that appear to address these in ways that we believe are "systemic enough" to qualify as methodology in this developing field.

The key issues we face seem to be connected more to the relationship between systemic working and the context of the large organization than to our characteristics as individual consultants. How can we meet the client's expectations of providing expert diagnosis and yet hold to our social construction-ist beliefs? How can we as often solo practitioners guard against falling into the positivist traps that we seek to help our clients avoid? Is it possible to integrate the power of the systemic method-ology with the traditions of organization development and other approaches to thinking about change in large systems? And, finally, how can we set up working relations with clients that are suffi-ciently results-orientated to persuade them it is worth working with us, while creating contexts that enable and support the far more open-ended, exploratory, and often confusing journey that real learning and second-order change requires?

Conventional approaches based on the "expert" stance to con-sulting suggest six or more stages that the consulting process moves through. Organization development and "process" approaches that have developed since use a similar model but add several extra stages to do with involving the client in the processes (Schein, 1987; Block, 1981). It is tempting, therefore, to think that a "systemic/ social constructionist" approach could be achieved by "bolting on" what people see as *the* new ideas, methods, and techniques that this approach seems to offer.

But as indicated in Chapter 2, the territory we move into with systemic working is very different from that inhabited by conven-tional providers of consulting advice. There is much more at stake when practitioners and their clients adopt this perspective—the very foundations of a lifetime of knowledge and expertise seem to be under threat. It seems to us that to make this move we are involved in a more complex process than the "bolting on" analogy suggests. We are creating and taking part in change at two levels:

1. the *identity* of the practitioner
2. the *context* in which the practitioner operates.

So in seeking to become constructionist consultants and manag-ers, we need to be not only working on a new sense of identity and new capabilities for ourselves, but also negotiating a relationship— a working context—with our clients that supports this new kind of identity and the thinking and behaviour that goes with it. In the next section, we look at some of the key elements of our constructionist consulting model. In the second section we outline some of the more practical steps we are taking to implement this evolving model, before moving on in the third part of the chapter to describe some constructionist processes that represent the emerging "technology" of our approach.

ELEMENTS OF A MODEL OF PRACTICE

Can we "use" systemic approaches, as in the sense of using a tool? Or, when we work systemically, do we have to cross a critical divide that separates "doing" from "being", behaviour from identity? And once we are "being systemic", are we so wholly immersed *in* the systemic mode that it is not realistic to think in terms of extricating ourselves sufficiently, to in any sense *use* particular aspects or techniques? This idea presents systemic novices and experienced practitioners alike with a major paradox: can we *be* systemic workers in organizational contexts in which we are usually being asked to *do*?

The key practical questions we have to deal with here in the context of our model are: is it possible to be in this position if the client and consulting context are firmly in the more conventional "linear" mode of thinking? And if this is problematic, is it possible to negotiate assignment contracts in which the focus can be on longer-term exploration and learning? Our experience in dealing with this paradox indicates that we need to work at resolving it at different levels. We find it useful to describe the model of the constructionist consulting that has emerged at three such levels (Dilts, Epstein, & Dilts, 1991): at what might be called the *identity* level (who do we think we are when we are doing this work?); at the level of the *beliefs, values, and principles* that we follow; and finally, at the level of the *strategies and capabilities* used.

The level of identity

For the constructionist consultant, the question of identity is a crucial one. Given the focus on relational phenomena and language, the concept of identity has to be unconventional. From an *interaction* point of view, it can be seen as one half of a *relationship* with a client or group of clients. Therefore, the actual sense of identity is very much dependent on the "other" with whom you are engaged, so the serious constructionist can be faced with a very chameleon-like existence during working hours! When we approach the question from the point of view of *language*, we might in a similar fashion understand individual identity very much as being located at the intersection of dynamic multiple **discourses** (see Glossary). Earlier comments on the thinking behind "observing systems" and "second-level cybernetics" seem to add support to this more complex way of thinking about who we are and might become.

For people like us who have learned to believe in the value of the constructionist approach, the road to internalizing this concept of professional identity has been a long and tricky one, and we have gradually come to a different understanding of how we as consultants are effective in our work.

- We see ourselves as a *part* of the systems we are engaged with, actively *constructing* a view of a problem with the client, and not as separate individuals on the fringe of client systems, who *discover* the problems that the clients are struggling with.

- We realize how important it is to give client groups an impression of *neutrality*, not taking sides with any particular view or person, if we are to encourage empowerment and a full expression of stakeholder interests.

- In maintaining this discipline of neutrality, we also have to learn that expressing our own views about the *content* of client problems is not always a useful option; often it is more effective to find other ways of using our own thoughts and feelings about the conflicts and dilemmas that arise in client situations, understanding these as *feedback* about how the system is responding—e.g. rather than giving a judgement on an argument between two people when appealed to, to ask others present what this argument might represent in the wider system.

- Finally we need to learn how to *live* this relational way when working in a professional capacity—it is a praxis, not a theory or technique—by being ready at all times to engage in *inquiry and dialogue* with clients about what is happening and what we are doing, no matter how challenging.

The repeated experience of being in this co-constructing relationship with clients and colleagues has created contexts that have allowed our identities as constructionist consultants to emerge. This has enabled us to hold an observer position to our relationship with others, which makes it possible for us to remain aware of *how we are being as we are doing*.

In line with the *discursive* concept of identity (Harré & Gillett, 1994) mentioned in the first paragraph of this section, we have found it useful to see ourselves as being at the nexus of a number of personal, social, and professional discourses. One of these is the client discourse where we have our ordinary views as just another participant in the on-going discussion. Another is the professional discourse of systemic and constructionist thinking, which can be foregrounded as and when it is appropriate. Using these different perspectives or positions allows us to move out of our neutral or *systemic* stance and take strong positions from time to time as our views dictate. However, as we do this we do not feel that once we have expressed such a *personal* view, we need to defend it as being *the* right construction of the situation. Instead we take care to *mark* this as a personal position, so that we can move fluently to a systemic position to hear the feedback in a more relational way.

This fluid, *oscillatory* process allows us to work in a flexible and often neutral way and yet also act with some authority when appropriate. This leads to an expression of constructionist consulting identity that may be called *authoritative diffidence*—meaning that while we are quite clear about what we think and feel, we continue to be both curious and irreverent (Cecchin, Lane, & Ray, 1992) about the outcomes that emerge from the interaction and our own particular role and contribution.

The level of beliefs and values

Supported by this view of identity are a number of beliefs and principles that guide and influence the way we see, think, and feel about the people and situations we work with. These have come out of our own experience as aspiring constructionist consultants but also are supported from the emerging literature that can be associated with this field. Key elements of this belief structure are:

• In human affairs, we believe in the interpretive idea of *multiple realities*; this does not preclude the idea of a single reality as such, but in this view it would need to be one that is *negotiated* between observers in a *local* context.

- In line with the idea of multiple and local realities, we believe there are many possible pathways forward to a goal or solutions to a problem; this idea chimes with the cybernetic concept of *equifinality*.

- To be of help as a consultant, it is absolutely critical to understand and work with the meaning of the picture or story that is held in the mind of the client; while this may be just *one* possible picture or story among many, without this intimate human *connection* between helper and client, we believe no real progress can be made.

- Clients often appear to resist ideas: we welcome such *"resistance"* and see it as a marker of important values and positive intentions; similarly, they may also give us the impression that they are struggling or stuck; again we don't take this as a sign that they lack the motivation or basic *abilities* to progress. In both instances, we believe it means they lack *choice* and would benefit from a particular experience in a particular context which will give them the information they need to take the next step.

- In line with the findings of Argyris (1990), we find that many of the issues that trouble organizations can be associated with the high value people place on *control* and the "skilled incompetence" that this appears to generate; in contradistinction, however, we find that genuine longer-term solutions to these problems are best tackled, not as matters of *individual* competence, but as problems embedded *in the language of the system* (or culture). These need to be re-solved by the *group* of people who, through their mutual interaction, are creating and maintaining a particular dynamic around the problem in focus.

The level of strategies and capabilities

Translating these more general ideas of identity and belief into the actions we can take to position and deliver a service takes us into the domain of strategy and capability. At this level there are many concepts and techniques we can employ, but in line with our earlier warning about the oversimplistic "bolt on" analogy, these need to be used congruently—that is, in alignment with the constructionist identity and beliefs expressed earlier. There is more on the model at this level of thinking in the next section on praxis development, but here we would like to identify what we consider to be some of the central ideas:

• We look and listen very carefully to understand the client's *own construction* of their context and problem. What is being picked out as significant? What is being left unsaid or glossed over? What are the key presuppositions and values that are embedded in the language they are using?

• We look further for *connections to other positions* and views that might be relevant, and seek to identify the "other sides" of presenting claims and concerns, and other poles of dilemmas, in order to challenge and enrich the client's maps.

• We challenge and question clients principally to initiate and generate a two-way *feedback* process; it is from this that a new understanding and new ideas will emerge.

• We suspend judgement for as long as we feel appropriate; we decide to intervene when we start to see *redundancy* in the process—that is, the client starts to go over old ground, or seems to be bored or stuck with one point of view.

• We continually use feedback to develop and update our *evolving hypotheses* about the meaning of behaviour in the system; when we feel the client is stuck or will benefit from moving on, we design activities and experiences that will *generate feedback* to test these hypotheses and so provide the client/consultant relationship with ideas as to next steps. These exercises are designed to help the client take up an *observer position* to their experience in order that they might understand this experience in a fresh context.

• We make full use of our *own feelings* and thoughts to generate hypotheses, ideas, and claims about how the system is working and how people feel about this (the second-level cybernetics position); we also take up a more *neutral* position where we seek to move away from the position of these *personal* views in order to understand feedback in all its forms, as relational and systemic phenomena. We see this *oscillatory process* as essential to being both engaged and "objective".

- Many problems in human systems are usefully approached as problems of communication about the ambiguities and conflicts that people face; when they are helped to get in touch again with the tensions of the underlying dilemmas (and associated losses and gains), they can be enabled to understand the many options and choices they have.

- When people are enabled to engage in open two-way *dialogue*, appropriate meanings and next-action steps for that context will *emerge*—there is no need or purpose in trying to control the interaction towards some predetermined end.

- Throughout the working process, we are seeking to identify issues at two levels: the *content* dilemmas that are leading to operating difficulties in the client system, and the *contextual* dilemmas that are preventing the client system from addressing these. We see our primary task to be the resolution of the latter, but to accomplish this task we may engage in dialogue about content dilemmas, context dilemmas, or both.

THE DEVELOPMENT OF A PRAXIS

In this section we turn to a description of the competencies and tactics that we use to express our practice within the outline model of consulting developed in the previous section. Our views are set out under what we see to be the three primary operational dimensions of this model of consultancy:

1. operating in the second-level cybernetics position;
2. generating and then using valid information to steer change processes;
3. supporting the creation of a praxis of learning.

Operating in the second-level cybernetics position

To work systemically, you, as manager and consultant, need first of all to take up a position in which you understand and act not as an objective observer of a problem, but as an active participant in a subjectively defined network of relationships formed around the problem. What you see is not *the* problem, but a constituent part of the problem. This requires an acceptance of and an ability to create contexts in which *local and relational forms of knowledge* are privileged. Using the principles of *universal to local knowledge* and *observed to observing systems* provides a new structure of thinking for the systemic worker. The enactment of these principles helps the manager or consultant create the kind of boundary conditions, working relationship, and contract that supports systemic work and covers those phases of consulting that are typically called the "entry", "contracting", and "exit" phases.

The initial two phases are the first practice problems that the aspiring constructionist consultant meets—how to gain entry in such a way that the foundations for constructionist working are laid explicitly, so that such working does not take place only behind the scenes or in the shadow. The following are some of the practical steps we take to create these enabling conditions:

- *Working pattern:* We find that a "little and often" approach encourages clients to take more responsibility themselves for moving the assignment forward. This pacing of our contacts gives the client system time to digest and make sense of the ideas generated during sessions, so that when we again work with the client, we will be dealing typically with the outcomes and *effects* of such interventions. This approach also supports a cycle of hypothesizing and strategizing, followed by action, with the effects then being reviewed later in the light of system feedback.

- *Sense of time:* Clients always experience a dilemma over the "urgent" versus "important" issue in defining priorities. We believe that change needs to take place at a variety of paces, and so we often deliberately play around with change and the related time scales in order to encourage a more differentiated view of the situation. So we may push for immediate progress in, say, how people go about understanding a problem, while proposing a much slower pace for the shared evolution of new work norms.

- *Contractual fees:* Many clients prefer us to work for a specific fee for a defined outcome of work. This is tidy but tends to

encourage us all to *act on* the system in order to deliver preor-
dained results. We find that better and more responsive work
can often be done when working to a retainer. Though there is a
danger that the work may then lack sufficient focus, we feel
able to join more effectively with clients in attending to the
meaning of feedback and seeking a proper balance between
action and reflection.

- *Strategy and learning:* With so much of the focus on making
  meaning in the present, there is always a danger that the work
  can get sidetracked or lose direction. To guard against this we
  usually try to negotiate a separate arrangement for an on-going
  role consultation with the most senior person in the relevant
  unit. Such work allows the client/consultant pair to work at
  two levels:

  1. on the here-and-now sense-making of the executive in his or
      her role—the reflexive learning aspect;
  2. on the direction and strategic progress being made by the
      unit for which he or she is responsible.

Generating valid information to steer change processes

Finding out what is construed as both valid and valuable requires
work with relevant *stakeholders,* who constitute problem-determined systems, and an ability to *inquire participatively*—often in
conditions of tension and conflict—to find out why people hold the
views that they do hold. This process benefits from an acceptance
of the principles of *part to whole* and *debate to dialogue.* A willingness
to suspend judgements about what to do and how to do it until
the *meaning of the feedback* has been reviewed and some form of consensus established is also critical. A belief in the efficacy of moving
from *detail to dynamic complexity* and *quantification to appreciation,*
allows practitioners to work more easily in this way.

This dimension of the model provides a means of constructing
valid systemic knowledge with clients and other stakeholders covering the consulting phases normally referred to as "diagnosis" and
"planning change". During this process the consultant helps client
systems try out different formulations of problem and solution, in
order to construct more effective levels of agreement about the

degree of fit with their intentions and the requirements of their local context. Some of the tactics we employ to assist this process include:

- *Everyday understanding:* It is very easy during assignments to give the impression that your own or senior management's views are more expert or relevant than those of "ordinary" organization members; as this is completely counter to the systemic view, we take great care to privilege what are sometimes called the everyday meanings and constructions that are employed by other people whose views typically get less attention by using, for example, focus groups, diagonal "slice" events involving people from several functions and levels, and so on.

- *Increasing requisite variety:* To ensure that it is not our own methods that limit the quality of dialogue and understanding, we are at pains to use a wide variety of communication media and means—e.g. metaphor, corporate myths, "right-brain" thinking, simulations, and roleplaying.

- *Pacing the inquiry:* Individuals, groups, and organizations take time to process the impact of interventions and for the meaning of the feedback to become clear. We prefer, therefore, to pace our own interventions so that the effects of one intervention are registered before another is started. This also allows us to expand slowly the scope of an inquiry to include all the relevant parties in a problem-determined system.

- *Maintaining "objectivity":* It is very easy to become "organized" by a client—i.e. become convinced by their point of view—and so lose effectiveness. To help us maintain our systemic perspective we make use of a number of mechanisms such as regular hypothesizing, "extra-vision" provided by colleagues not involved in the assignment, and personal strategies to elicit ongoing states of curiosity and irreverence.

Supporting the creation of a praxis of learning

Learning to be more effective in organizations is essentially an active process. New knowledge (the "whats") and associated practices (the "hows") emerge from action and interaction as people find new ways of relating and new meanings in what they are doing together. What is required is a context and the appropriate means for facilitating and validating such "learning in action", as people strive together to achieve agreed aims. Such active learning processes are more easily created when practitioners move the working relationship from one based on *instruction* to *interaction* and understand their interventions not as *instruments* for change but as *processes* for learning.

Once the learning process has been activated, it becomes clearer that the meaning(s) of what is done comes primarily from how those involved understand their local contexts. Furthermore, people generally respond more genuinely not to what others say but to what they *do*. Creating the conditions for such local interaction presupposes that people will have opportunities to meet face to face with others to negotiate both the content and meaning of the issues that affect them. Favouring the *oral* mode of communication over the *literal*, and emphasizing *enactment* over *espousal* during change processes, raises people's awareness of the contextual issues involved and helps them engage in discourse at the critical level of identity.

These types of processes can occur at any time during an assignment but match the "intervention" and "feedback/evaluation" stages of the conventional consulting cycle. In our view, second-order change and the so-called ability of organizations to learn both depend heavily on consultants and clients making greater use of these more open-ended, fluid, and exploratory processes than is usually the case in current practice. As with the other dimensions of the constructionist model, we should emphasize that these describe attributes of *working relations* rather than the abilities of individuals. Some of the practices we use to create working contexts in which this can happen include:

- *Model of communications:* To encourage our clients to take seriously their power to influence the future, we continually emphasize the relevance of the "emergent" model of communication (as against the "pipeline" model which encourages passivity—see Reframe 9 in Chapter 2 for more details). As they are already exercising a degree of responsibility for and influence over what is going on in the present, we point out that it is not such a leap of faith to think more positively about changes they could aspire to in the future.

- *New narratives:* The ability of many client organizations to change is severely restricted by staff acceptance of myths that limit their scope for personal choice and empowerment. In these situations we spend time helping them explicate these myths and identify the many exceptions where they and others have found it possible to act counter to the apparently all-powerful story (White, 1991). It then becomes possible to bring to the foreground other more enabling versions of the myth, and to make the new connections between centre and periphery that are needed to provide support for and affirm these more empowering stories.

- *Hologram effect:* As changes start to percolate down the hierarchy and ideas start crossing old divides, we ourselves take time to raise the visibility of evidence that signals the emergence of a new coherence in the organization. The purpose of these dialogues is to help people recognize and reconstruct with each other that quality of connectedness that is characterized by the metaphor of the hologram. In organizations this is usually seen in terms of vision and values, structure and policies, and the processes used to manage the inside and outside and can be recognized in the mind-maps carried by individual staff, in the way groups work, and in how different functions relate to each other, to customers, and to other outside groupings.

- *Observer perspective:* A major preoccupation throughout any assignment is to keep shifting our angle of view so that the client is continually being gently challenged to reflect on the meaning of their actions and the effects these induce. The purpose of this "dance" is to help the client learn to move between content and process, between identity and context, and between what Argyris (1990), calls "single-loop learning" and "double-loop learning". As people learn to make these shifts themselves, the organization begins to develop the capacity to become a learning organization.

AN EVOLVING METHODOLOGY

Within the practice framework outlined above, we have found it possible to use a number of intervention patterns that seem compatible and effective in helping clients make progress (or, paraphrasing Wittgenstein, 1958, know how to take the next step). As illustrations of current methodology, we now offer brief descriptions of approaches that we feel we have used successfully enough times for these to qualify as elements of a developing methodology within which we find we can be "systemic enough". At the present time, there are six main "interventions" that fit these criteria. Readers will be able to recognize references to these approaches in earlier chapters, especially in the extended case studies in Chapters 3, 4, and 5.

"The FORESEE® approach"— negotiating learning partnerships

Systemic practitioners come up against the greatest difficulties at the very beginning of potential assignments. At this stage the consulting context and the consultant's natural tendencies are pushing towards expert and non-systemic lines of approach, which in the longer term are likely to be self-defeating. To create a container for initial discussions between client and consultant that encourages a different working relationship in which constructionist work can flourish, we have developed a four-step process, the FORESEE® approach (a pun on the *four C's* that label the four steps in the process; see Figure 5):

- *Connecting:* At the very beginning of a discussion, the prime focus needs to be on establishing genuine connections between client and consultant. Given the different contexts that the two come from, there is an immediate problem of translation—to what extent are we using words and concepts that have a common meaning? When talking to, say, German or French people, it is easy to be conscious of the likely differences between us, but not when we seem to be speaking the same language. So this first phase is very much about creating a "conversational protocol" in which it becomes natural to explore the possible

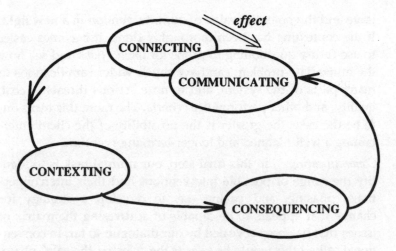

Figure 5.   **The FORESEE® approach to selling**

meanings of issues and ideas. From this it is more likely that a shared understanding of the *situation* faced by the "client-and-consultant" system can emerge, with both parties clear about the reasons for their work together.

• *Contexting:* Once the general frame for our discussion has been established it is natural to move towards understanding the particular *problem* in more detail. In this finding-out phase, we use hypothesizing and circular questioning to expand our mutual understanding of the system in which the problem exists: Who is most interested in this issue? What are the different views that compete for legitimation? How do the stakeholders go about pursuing their claims and concerns? With what effect? This exploratory process helps both client(s) and ourselves to develop a rich picture of why the problem persists and how various parties are "co-operating" to maintain this situation.

• *Consequencing:*   This often appears to be the most critical phase in the process: What is likely to happen if the current trend continues and nothing changes? This is where the performance and financial ramifications of a no-change scenario start to emerge, and where the client, in particular, starts to look at the issue and the potential value of our intervention in a new light. If the contexting has been thoroughly done, it becomes easier to use future questioning to probe for *implications* and see how the immediate problem can have much wider ramifications in many parts of the system, and to pose serious threats to cost, quality, and other performance criteria. The more this turns out to be the case, the greater is the possibility of the client entertaining a well-planned and longer-term intervention.

- *Communicating:* In this final step, our mutual task is to identify the range of possible interventions and their interconnections, phasing, and pacing—i.e. to develop a strategy for change that appears to be capable of addressing the matrix of issues that has been revealed by our dialogue so far. In conventional selling this would be seen as the "closing-the-sale" phase, and there clearly are many similarities between the two (Rackham, 1987). The differences that have an important effect on the quality of the process we establish with clients are:

  - the shaping of "offer" to fit "need" is done by both the client and consultant as a mutual strategy of intervention evolves—i.e. it is a *joint* construction;

  - this strategy (or set of linked interventions) is one that involves both the client and consultant in separate *and* joint activity; the "closing of the sale" therefore is not to do just with defining the consultant's separate contribution, but with the work that *both* client and consultant are "buying into" together;

  - the value of attending to context and mutual inquiry into the meaning of feedback establishes a level of dialogue that ensures that any ensuing contract is clearly founded on a culture of continuous learning and adaptation; in other words, in "closing the sale" we are agreeing to evolve continually the substance of the sale.

We find that this four-step process is very demanding in terms of time, mental effort, and faith in clients to play fair with us—after all, we are often delivering a lot of our best work in this pre-contract phase. However, given the "invisible" nature of our service, we find that this process offers potential clients a practical demonstration of what our constructionist service is actually about and, often enough, leads to satisfying and productive long-term relations.

"Role consultation"— *strategic thinking for top managers*

A major outcome of the constructionist approach is reflexive learning in context. This supports a dynamic and responsive approach to change: each step is subjected to a searching scrutiny on its effects (rather than the intent behind it), through engaging in dialogue with stakeholders about the meaning of feedback. However, what this approach often lacks in work with large organizations is a sense of strategy—that is, organization-wide thinking and longer-term plans for change. How can an outside consultant engage with an organization in a way in which both strategic intent and responsiveness to feedback can be addressed?

We have found that role-analysis– or role-consultation–type approaches can be very useful here, particularly when these are with chief executive level managers. The general approach has been around for some time (e.g. see Reed, 1976) and in essence is a process of working one-to-one over a period of time with an executive to explicate their idea of role and to understand the current dynamics of relations with adjacent roles. What we now add to this process are the constructionist and observing systems perspectives. What we find is that if the executive in question occupies a very senior position in the organization, the exploration of role often also serves as a proxy analysis of the organization's vision, mission, and values. And in this type of application, it can act as a mechanism for integrating strategic thinking with responsiveness to on-going feedback.

We often combine this with the FORESEE® process as a way of starting a relationship with an organization. This establishes a pattern where we can work in an exploratory way with an executive first to identify intentions, develop strategy, and design and rehearse interventions and then, at a later session, to review feedback to establish impact and meaning. This then naturally leads into the next cycle of action-based learning, and so can become a regular part of a process of "steering" change, helping senior executives clarify the role they need to take up in the process. This approach can also be very useful in the development of senior executives. In helping executives think through and then address various dilemmas and difficulties over time, the process provides a natural and practical introduction to systemic and constructionist methods, giving them a range of opportunities to integrate these ideas into their own perspective.

The early part of the case in Chapter 5 provides a good example of how we use this approach (in combination with others) at the start of an assignment. In this instance, we used the process to initiate conversations in which both the reflexive learning and strategic change criteria could be met. Our work with Gordon, the top executive in the organization, continually straddled both of these dimensions so that when our one-to-one work with him helped him reach certain conclusions as to how he should proceed on a personal basis, we were also in fact engaged with the strategic aspects of the proposed changes.

"Participative inquiry"—identifying the real differences

Where the client is prepared to consider a more far-reaching and long-term exploration process in order to surface options for future strategic development, we can adopt a more research-orientated perspective. To effect this we use an inquiry-orientated consulting style, designed to promote a more organic exploration of the views of people involved in the particular issue, and an outcome that more truly represents a consensus.

These participative research methods represent a break with the long-unquestioned reliance on scientific/positivist methods that have been so successful in the physical sciences (Lincoln & Guba, 1985; Reason, 1988). Though sometimes confused with qualitative methods of research, they do in fact spring out of the wholly different *relativist* paradigm. Used mainly in policy-evaluation studies in the educational world, this approach is based on a subjectivist **epistemology** (see Glossary) that unites "knower" and "known" and brings together the researcher and all stakeholders in an interaction that *creates* the product of the evaluation. This is in marked contrast to conventional methods, where the product is specified *before* the research starts. The key dynamic is the use of carefully controlled negotiation between all stakeholders to identify fully the level of consensus around the various concerns, claims, and issues that together are energizing and maintaining a particular dynamic in the system. This leads to enfranchising and empowering many groups of people who, because they do not usually have a say either in policy formulation or its implementation, misunderstand or resist the changes that the organization needs to make.

In line with our general constructionist approach, this method pays a great deal of attention to the influence of *context* on the meanings people attribute to ideas and issues. While a salesman and a colleague in the production department may appear to be using the same meaning for, say, the word "quality", we often find that this apparent easy consensus leads to more confusion than if they were speaking different languages. It is the *local* contexts from which they speak and into which they speak that determine the specific meanings they are employing, and it is here that the differences need to be systematically teased out and examined by both parties to ensure mutual understanding. This level of open dialogue is seldom possible in the normal course of events, and the participative inquiry process provides a discipline and climate in which such *mutual construction* of local realities can take place.

The typical process adopted in such assignments covers the following:

- Identifying the full range of stakeholders who might be at risk, involved, or have interests in the outcome of the project; this is not a once-off activity, as the process itself is open to the inclusion of further interested parties as the research proceeds.

- Eliciting from all stakeholders their insider constructions about the primary theme, and the claims, concerns, and issues they wish to raise in relation to it. This step usually identifies a number of subgroups who appear to share similar constructions, and these are formed into what Guba and Lincoln (1989) call "hermeneutic circles" (or meaning-making groups).

- Assisting the subgroups to understand and critique the claims, concerns, and issues that their members share, and then to cross-fertilize these discussions with the constructions developed by the other subgroups.

- Generating consensus to as many constructions and their related claims, concerns, and issues as possible, first within subgroups and then between subgroups. Once a consensus has been achieved, the item can be dropped from the dialogue.

- Preparing an agenda and facilitating negotiations within and between subgroups on the constructions where there is an incomplete consensus or none. The role of the facilitator in these situations is to identify the new information that might lead to the resolution of competing constructions, and where possible to provide participants with this information in an appropriate format.

- Documenting the outcomes that have been achieved. This is usually provided in the form of a narrative or case study, as this seems to be the most effective way of representing the views of stakeholders and preserving the contextual underpinnings that have led to these new agreements and any continuing disagreements.

The development agenda work referred to in Reframe 3 in Chapter 2 is a good example of how we use this approach. A series of initial exploratory discussions with each of the members of the team was followed by further one-to-one reviews in which key differences between parties were further investigated. The emerging consensus about issues that would benefit from a more developmental approach was then documented in a narrative form, and subjected to detailed critique by the participants in functional subgroups and then in the group as a whole. By the end of this process, there was a shared view of the need for a more developmental approach to certain issues and mutual understanding of where people were holding different constructions. This groundwork allowed the group to make rapid progress on a range of issues that had been causing difficulties for over a year.

"Whole group working"—facilitating system-wide dialogue

To initiate change in problem-determined systems, we work with the whole system using a process not unlike search conferences (Weisbord, 1990). The purpose that underlies the design, however, is different in that we focus more strongly on introducing ideas of context and of circularity. In these events, structure and process facilitation is provided by the consultants, with the content of issues and expertise in the business coming from the *whole* participant group, not just from the specialists on the management team. The events are usually held away from the place of work, often over weekends, creating a sense of "time out of time", which supports the encouragement of right-brain, pictorial, dramatic, and allegorical methods of communicating. The emphasis of the event throughout is towards creating a supportive climate in which oral modes of communication and interaction can flourish, thus making visible to participants the reflexive connections between context, behaviour, and meaning.

The vignette included in Reframe 2 in Chapter 2 illustrates one use of this approach. Another is the main intervention in the case in Chapter 5. This shows how important the positioning of such events is—they would not be nearly so effective without the "connecting and fitting" activities that we engage in prior to the event itself. It also indicates how the design of such apparently "standard" approaches does in fact *emerge* from the hypothesizing activity about the *local context* that takes place between client and consultant. Finally, it illustrates the need for consultants using this method to be operating out of the constructionist perspective: using this method as a tool to "sell" management ideas to staff— as an "expert" consultant might—would lead to very different results.

"Development programmes"—improving management praxis

Our approach is different when the client's concern is more with the second phase of implementing change, following the initial high-profile "training cascade" or "visioning" change workshops. Here we evolve with the client a development programme, sometimes comprising several modules, aimed at supporting groups of managers to make the connection between new ideas and their local experience. We ground the programmes in the managers' current change accountabilities and specifically build in the trialling of new learning and its reinforcement through reflection on the meaning of the feedback experienced by the manager during the second phase.

A good illustration of this approach occurred as a consequence of the work we touched on in the short case described in Reframe 4 in Chapter 2. Following this top management workshop we were asked to develop a programme for the top 100 managers from the two merging agencies, to help them deal with a long-drawn-out period of uncertainty as the proposed changes were approved by the Government. By using the development-programme format of *thinking/trialling/adapting to feedback*, we were able to engage the participants and help them shift from an all-or-nothing, un-differentiated, and essentially disempowering view of the situation. Instead, in conjunction with their new colleagues-to-be, they were enabled to identify, try out, and then commit to a variety of short-term initiatives that were likely to fit into the envelope of feasible strategic options that the organization was considering.

"The generative cascade"—towards organization learning

In large organizations, effective change requires the active involvement of managers and staff at many levels. This takes time and is subject to considerable filtering—from the natural distortion that affects everyday communication to the more systemic effects that take place as people respond to the contradictions they see between what managers say and what they actually do. To overcome this dissipation of focus and energy, top management often employ very structured, high-profile, intensive training programmes, the so-called training "cascade" (Figure 6). Through these they hope to inculcate a whole new way of working throughout an organization in a very short period of time. Unfortunately, most of these attempts appear not to deliver their promise, and they soon need to be reinforced with other programmes.

We have spent some time developing a process that can provide the "simple solutions to complex problems" approach that seems to be required, but one that can also address the multiple subcultures and local contexts that characterize the large, diverse organization. We have adopted the "cascade" idea as a useful metaphor for the process involved but have adapted it to the demands of the second-order level of change that so many organizations are now seeking. In this version, the cascade is not understood as being primarily about knowledge and behaviour

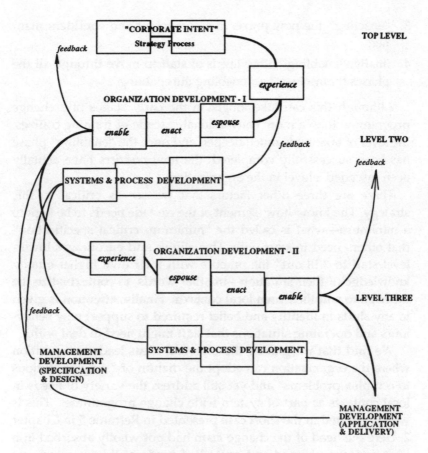

Figure 6. **The generative cascade**

transfer, but about the quality of relations between manager and staff. What needs to cascade down the organization is a different relational process that models and embodies the "new way" in its fullest sense.

Obviously, this means that each level in the hierarchy has to move through several developmental phases before the "new way" can be enacted and properly transferred to the next responsible level of staff. We see these phases as four in number, with considerable overlap between each:

1. "experiencing" the new way for oneself;
2. "espousing" the new ideas and practices;

3. "enacting" the new praxis in a competent and confident manner;

4. finally, "enabling" other levels of staff to move through all the phases themselves, i.e. "enabling the enabling".

Although this can take longer in the early stages of a change programme than a more conventional cascade of training courses, the level of take-up is much deeper, and once the "enabling" phase has been successfully completed, the new *practices* have actually been cascaded a level in the organization.

There are three other factors that we see as critical to this strategy. The know-how element of the cascade needs to be kept to a minimum—what is called the "minimum critical specification" that others need to start with. This allows and encourages lower-level staff to "fill out" the practice with their own higher-quality knowledge of their situation—in other words, to contextualize the message to suit their own local contexts. Finally, attention is given to any shifts in identity and belief required to support new behaviours and operating situations that staff might need to deal with.

We find that integrating these several ideas leads to a position where the organization can adopt the dictum of "simple solutions to complex problems" and yet still address the variety of needs in local contexts as part of system-wide change programmes. This is well illustrated in the short case presented in Reframe 5 in Chapter 2. Here the head of the change team had got wholly absorbed into the top-down planned and controlled mode of thinking and was finding it increasingly difficult to pay any attention at all to the meaning of the negative feedback that was starting to build up as his programme cascaded downwards. Our reframing of the cascade concept allowed him to maintain the *idea* of a cascade structure to the programme but start to inject some circularity, feedback, and responsiveness into the process.

CONCLUDING THOUGHTS

In this chapter we have tried to convey our picture of what appears to us to be an emerging methodology for offering constructionist consulting in organizations. It is as yet ill-formed and sketchy, but we feel that this is probably inevitable in the context in which we are working. In large and complex organizations, it is much more difficult to be clear about the impact one is making on the whole system, and it also takes much longer to see any effects. More usually, one is working with just one group, a subcomponent of the whole system, where change is unlikely to quickly, if ever, change the whole organization's behaviour, and where attempts at change are likely anyway to shift the nature and focus of problems onto other subsystems.

There is another aspect of the approach that makes it difficult to pin down—the intimate involvement of the practitioners themselves. While we may have talked about lists of principles, tactics, and techniques in this chapter, it should be clear from what has gone before that these can only be regarded as constructionist "tools" when they are being used by someone who is actually practising the constructionist approach. Like high-quality cuisine, the recipes, culinary implements, and foodstuffs of constructionist consulting are nothing special without the presence of the master constructionist chef. Given the central importance of the identity, beliefs, and capabilities of the practitioner in this approach, we turn in the next two chapters to a consideration of what might be involved in taking up the practice of constructionist manager or consultant.

CHAPTER 7

Getting started

*Gaining acceptance of constructionist work
in an organizational context*

This chapter is most obviously relevant to those practising as external
management consultants. However, it may be equally valuable for internal consultants and managers acting in the role of "change agents".
For anyone "out of the line", putting themselves forward as a "helper",
there seem to be three stages to getting started: first, there is getting to be
seen; second, there is getting to be heard (at more than a superficial
level); and, finally, but often overlooked, there is the stage of getting to be
valued, without which there is no on-going basis for the helping relationship. For the external consultant, the first stage, getting to be seen, is more
difficult than for those helpers on the "inside". However, if the internal
"helper" is coming from the constructionist position, then many of the
problems associated with trying to start a conversation with someone who
expects directions are similar. For the "internal" helper, the problem may
turn on their being too well known, in the sense of their having some
preexisting relationship towards the problem system derived from their
place in the organization structure. From their different angles, both
internal and external consultants are trying to establish an optimum
distance between themselves and the problem system.

W hat do consultants do when they have found effective means of helping clients discover their own solutions to tough problems, but then find that their way of thinking is difficult to communicate because the prevailing alternative on offer is a universal prescription, packaged, easy to install, and, above all, so much more visible than the constructionist approach? Some of the means that we have discovered over the past few years are explored in this chapter.

GETTING TO BE SEEN— PACKAGING THE "INVISIBLE PRODUCT"

The first major hurdle, getting to be seen, is perhaps more of a challenge for systemic constructionist consultants than ordinary management consultants. Our problem is in maintaining a consistency of approach even from the very first contact. If our approach is about facilitating the emergence of new understanding through dialogue, how is it possible to gain attention without making statements, without falling into the linear communication mode that is implicit in most marketing media?

What, then, are the means that we use to try to escape this bind? Early on we realized that we had to use the conventional "channels" of communication, but in an adapted form so that the constructionist "flavour" of our service would be apparent. We had to fine-tune that adaptation so that the difference was not sufficient to confuse or deter potential clients from making contact. We had to start a conversation with prospective clients initially remote from us, and somehow give them the feeling that they knew enough about us to feel that there would be some gain from sharing the outline of a current problem or change issue with us. In a phrase, **meta-complementarity** (see Glossary) was a key. In our marketing, it worked in some of the following ways.

First, there was the question of product definition and sales support material. How could we package an interaction process?

How could we put a conversation into a brochure? We thought this had to be by creating an alternative punctuation to the norm of the marketplace. We set out to make the *whole* marketing and selling process an intervention that would in itself add value for the client organization. We integrated our marketing material with the succeeding selling and assignment negotiation phases. In other words, we aimed to put ourselves forward as if we were already in a consulting relationship with the cold-call "target". So although we maintained meta-complementarity with our prospective clients and competitors by producing a brochure, its content was linked to issues that we had picked up from the management press and from our conversations with managers. This "first side of a conversation" is what we pick up and continue in the brochure copy (see Figure 7), making explicit that we are looking for the response that will complete the *"conversational triplet"* and lead to a joint exploration of problems and to an intervention.

However, without some relevant connection to the clients' context the approach does not work. So we do not think of the brochure as something that can stand alone in carrying us into conversation with the prospective client. We research the situation of the client, firm, and industry in order to form a hypothesis about the nature of a context that might influence the meaning that the receiver makes of our initial statements in the brochure. We reflect this hypothesis in our covering letters, which are therefore specific to each potential client. The letter and the brochure combined have to convey a sense of relevant difference, but not too much, so that the client will be interested enough to agree to a face-to-face meeting and give us a real chance to begin a dialogue—a conversation where we can be influenced by and can affect the client system.

The "product" shifts rapidly to the background as we move into what other suppliers would regard as the selling task. For us, selling is another consultation that is intended to be helpful to the client organization in framing a different understanding of their problem and accepting the value of continuing the consultation, often by drawing in a wider representation of the "problem system". We structure this "selling" conversation carefully (as described later in this chapter) and supplement it at stages with additional material aimed at stimulating further reflection by the

King's
CONSULTING PARTNERS

The shape and content of this brochure reflect our attempt to resolve a particular consulting dilemma we face: no serious consultation is ever sold from a brochure, but can a serious consultancy sell its services without one?

Moreover, a brochure can only be one half of a communication. So it's not the best medium for us to convey fully the essence of our type of consultation, that free flow of conversation from which we construct with the client a mutual understanding of need and define the consulting intervention that meets it.

This relationship of consultant and client is particularly helpful with chronic performance problems and the difficult implementation phase that follows major corporate change strategies. Here **dilemmas** *and their resolution lie at the heart of management work.*

Resolving *dilemmas requires dialogue, enlisting the active contribution of those involved, accepting their differing values and priorities. There is no such thing as the 'one best solution' in business and people management. Effective managers take account of everyone's 'best solution' to forge even better ones that all can recognize. From such processes, practical solutions emerge which fit the local situation.*

In reading these pages each of you will make your own sense of what we have written. We hope that some of you will be interested enough to respond with the other half of this conversation, related to an issue you are seeking to resolve. From such dialogue we know previous clients gained added value and improved their competitive capability.

Figure 7. **The first side of a conversation**

client; for example, articles we have written, or position papers that record in more depth one of the subjects raised in the meeting. These are meant to provide another perspective on the client's issue and to trigger a willingness on their part to look at new options for the consulting relationship beyond their usual experience.

GETTING TO BE HEARD—
PATTERNS OF CONSULTANT/CLIENT CONNECTION

There are broadly two routes to a consulting relationship with a client organization. In the first, the potential client has a clear notion of what they want to achieve. "We invite tenders for the provision of change management consultancy. . . ." The "what" of this requirement is often spelled out in terms of reference, and sometimes the means as well. Consultants then compete on price and some attempt at service differentiation to secure the contract.

In the second route, the client is sure only that they are somehow dissatisfied with some aspect of current performance. They may not even have committed themselves to seeing it as a problem. Here, the key is for the consultant to have already built a relationship of interest and respect with the potential client, so that only one or possibly two are competing for the client's ear. In this context, something like a conversation becomes possible from which meaning can be jointly created, each agreeing that they are seeing the same event in the same way. The task of the consultant is to extend this agreement to include the means of making a difference to the problem situation.

The tendering trap

In the "product" route to getting heard, the trap for the constructionist consultancy is of being too clear about their different approach, creating a **symmetrical relationship** (see Glossary) with the client before the assignment has been awarded. In these situations, we have found it helpful to follow the principle that *if you push too soon or too hard for difference, your counterpart will emphasize stability, whereas if you join with them, you stand a better* *chance of influencing them to see the advantages of change.* So we accept the language the client uses and the framework they see as necessary for a good change intervention. However, we hope the client will experience, from the manner of our presentation and in the plans we make for the running of the programme within that framework, that there is a difference between us and more conventional consultancies.

This does not mean that we never "take a position" in our first interactions with potential clients. Where we have a hunch that acting in a particular way will generate feedback that will be useful to the client, we will recommend a course of action to the client. This may well involve us in accepting some preconceived preference of the client's. Sometimes we respond in this way because the client has involved us *because* they are aware of their system's need for some different experiences or inputs.

In the more usual situation, however, we try by our interaction with the client system to provide an experience of our difference. In the case of a financial services company, we followed the client's expectations by conducting a round of interviews with key executives. The expectation was that these would provide "information" from which a "diagnosis" could be made, which would inform the detail of the consulting programme we were being asked to tender for. We instead used the interviews as the start of a consultation, using hypotheses to guide questioning about differences around the subject of the tender—the introduction of a quality initiative. In the "beauty parade", we produced what was in effect an extended "intervention", built around our early systemic hypothesis, formed from these interviews. We drew out the dilemmas we perceived for different parts of their system to show how they created the problem. This showed very clearly how we arrived at our ideas for the content of the predetermined assignment framework that our client had provided.

To show that this story is not in the realm of fantasy, we admit that we did not "win" the assignment. We fell into the trap, in the last part of our presentation, of being too explicit about the novelty of our approach, without the time to provide an experience of the approach in action. The decision group was left confused and feeling insecure—no basis for establishing a new client relationship. Our consolation prize was the feedback from the Personnel Director, who had set up the tendering process. "You should avoid beauty parades—your approach is much too special to stand a chance. But I am amazed at what you found out about our system—you've started something moving, without even getting the assignment!"

The cascade catch

There is a variant of the *tendering trap* in which the difficulty for the constructionist consultant is that the client has firm ideas about the preferred strategy for change. Such opportunities often result from another piece of consultancy work by a "strategy boutique", which has produced a clear prescription of the critical success factors or changes in culture needed to secure strategic advantage. Whether internally or consultancy-produced, these prescriptions seem to the clients to raise the need for management activity: a clearly pre-mapped, sequenced change programme that will "deliver" the new culture. The client envisages a mix of instruction in new skills and of "communication" about the vision behind the new strategy.

For example, we have learned how to construct "change products" that can be fitted into a change plan and that do not appear too different from standard management language about change, competency constructs, and management skills and techniques. These products work at the systemic level, however, because we use people's actual work and change experiences as our content. We facilitate their ability to resolve these by acting on and responding to their network of working relationships.

We also add to the client's conception of the change cascade further stages designed to move the system from *first-* to *second-order change*. The standard instructive cascade tends to produce compliance at best, but often with varying levels of covert-to-overt resistance which mean that senior management have to maintain considerable pressure to sustain the new behaviour from the organization. Very many surveys of change programmes have reported disappointment with the sustainability, the "shelf-life" of new behaviour, while others report that the planned degree of change is never achieved. To get to the second order of change, we have identified a form of cascade that takes people beyond the knowledge transfer aspects of change to *enactment*, to *enabling* others to become involved in the change, and, finally, to what we call *enabling the enabling*—the manager facilitating self-managed change in staff in response to feedback in their system.

The demand for diagnosis

This second route to "being heard" is the one that offers most scope for the strategy we have developed for "being seen". The image that we think many potential clients have in mind is of a patient/ doctor relationship, where the patient is unclear what is causing a feeling of ill-health and hopes an expert will be able diagnose and prescribe a treatment. With such a starting point, the relationship is more conducive to a constructionist approach.

For the consultant, the danger lies in falling in too easily with the pacing expectation that the patient/doctor model might create. The trap is the belief that something concrete has to be specified in order for a sale to occur. The pressure is to fit in with the linear view and specify as well as quantify the form of a possible assignment in a costed proposal linked to a timescale of activity.

The more helpful frame we strive to establish with the client is that of mutual agreement about the value of continuing a conversation, for which some rate of payment is acceptable to both sides. What we try to achieve is a shift to a frame where the oral mode is preferred to the literary, and appreciative criteria to the quantified. The agreement we reach may be firm for no further forward than the next meeting or agreed event. We may agree to put forward some options for further progress beyond that, but they will only be general and not specified tightly enough to form a contract. They will be clearly linked to a hypothesis that "we will find it worthwhile at that time to do the following sort of work".

In new client situations, we set out deliberately to follow our FORESEE® process in the conversation (see Chapter 6). We plan extensive use of questioning in order to elicit from the customer an explicit statement of needs whose economic importance has been assessed. In constructionist terms, this initial sequence of questioning serves to establish the *context* of the problem. We focus particularly on clarifying the *relationships* that have formed to bring forth the problem in the form of the difficulties or dissatisfactions of the present situation. At this point, our hypothesizing usually makes it possible to discern certain implied needs, but we realize that it would be easy to fall into the trap of starting too soon to put forward aspects of our product/service that would meet these needs. There is a further stage to go through before this active selling stance is appropriate.

This is to do with the effects or *consequences* of the existence of the client's problems. These expose the dynamics of various past and future options for resolving the problem. The benefits of our collaborative approach really come to the fore at this stage as the gains and/or losses of change for the various parts of the problem system are surfaced and explored. This helps both sides to understand the value or importance of a solution to all the parts of the client's problem system. This gives a much more precise statement of needs and priorities, which enables us to gauge better the "product" we should put forward and the price-band within which we can manoeuvre. It helps, of course, that the client too has developed a stronger sense of the cost-benefit of using our services. Approached in this way, the selling conversation can often be concluded with an intervention that fits with the understanding gained by the client system but reframes the issue that needs attention.

What is particularly interesting is our experience that this conversation may not take place all at a single time, but may sometimes be spread over a month or more.The "closure" of the selling process therefore comes as both consultant and client agree that a difference is beginning to be made to the problem system. A proposal may well have been prepared, more because that is what is expected in the market-place. The major benefit is that this records the shared understanding of the context that has developed, specifies fairly precisely what could be the next steps, but only outlines what might be most helpful beyond that. Over-defining the proposal would transgress our belief in structure-determined change and **dissipative structures** (see Glossary)—the essentially unpredictable and sudden evolution of radical shifts that occur when you "give the client system a bump".

Our experiences in "getting to be heard" have been helped by reflecting upon our own dilemma: how can I *be* a systemic consultant in situations in which I am being asked to reassure someone how I will go about *doing* something? We have realized that one can be in *both* positions, provided that one does not try to combine them *at the same time*. We can be in a "linear thinking" mode at one stage of the selling sequence and then deal with the feedback from that stage using systemic thinking. For example, rather than defending some recommendation we had made earlier, we try to understand what the reaction from elsewhere in the client system tells us about the meaning of change, at this time, or in this way, in different parts of the client system. This learning has reinforced our awareness that "being systemic" is just one punctuation of our experience as consultants; our systemic practice can equally be seen as a series of smaller linear episodes, of stimulus and response. The gain from this resolution of the dilemma is that we can use *all* our resources—our former experiences and ways of understanding, as well as our systemic lenses—when these will help us avoid getting stuck in certain traps.

Influencing the hierarchy

At this point, readers who are *not* designated as change agents in their system may be wondering whether there is any relevance of constructionist thinking for them in their situation, embedded within an organizational hierarchy. They do not have the "luxury" of the external consultant's mandate to effect change. They may, however, be just as interested in trying to influence a shift in "the way things are done around here", simply because they are committed to their organization's success. In our work, we have consulted to many people in such positions, and we outline below a step-by-step guide for one exercise which has enabled "internal consultants" to promote change in their own organizations.

> *Exercise E:* First, think of one area of work that you feel is not satisfactory, and for which you think change might be helpful. If you put this forward to your boss, what do you think will be his reaction, from what you "know" of him? And what might be the reactions of other managers who are particularly influential with your boss, or whose attitudes/actions have an effect on his ability to achieve his objectives? What might your boss be want-

ing to show those others by the surmised stance he would take towards your change idea and the "status quo"? Similarly what might their reactions to possible change be meant to show to your boss? Can you see any connections between the components of this system you have hypothesized around the problem issue?

Second, be aware of *your own place* in this problem system. What are you trying to show and to whom particularly by making your change suggestion? How is your suggestion affected by what you know of the views of others, not necessarily those you have already hypothesized are part of the problem system? In other words, we are prompting you to think of how you yourself may be being "organized" by a wider system of influences. This may be a particularly difficult step to take without the help of a "buddy" to bounce your thoughts off and to challenge you.

Next, it might be helpful to think of your boss as "meat in a sandwich" (see Campbell et al., 1991a). What might there be in your proposal that creates a dilemma for him? What aspects of his beliefs (about being a manager/boss/colleague/loyal employee of the firm etc.) would make it easy for him to accept the proposal and what difficult? When you have a sense of this dilemma, think carefully about the losses and gains of each side of the position he must feel himself in. If he were to put one side of this set of beliefs before others (privileging one set of values), what would this enable him to do; equally what would it enable him to avoid doing? Then you can extend this thinking, and try to see what are related sets of dilemmas, each with their own losses and gains, for the other members of the problem system.

The next step is holistic in its treatment of your problem. Instead of thinking only about acting to reduce the factors that you see contrary to your proposition, we suggest you think about a different way of viewing the issue, which would allow other beliefs of other people involved to be equally "privileged". This involves being flexible about your own proposition, in which you may only see the advantages of your way of resolving the dilemma behind the issue. What other possible ways can you see of addressing the issue, and what effect would these different ways have on the other members of the problem system?

How could you suggest formulating the issue that would help your boss to shift *without* having to reject one of the "cluster of contexts" he is trying to balance (see Figure 2 in Chapter 1). And what action could you suggest that would not negatively connote (see Glossary, **negative connotation**) his previous position?

What you will probably find if you stick to this set of exercises is that your experience of interactions, your style of communicating, will shift. You will probably become more interested in others, questioning at a deeper (but not necessarily personal) level than usual. You will tend to open out subject discussions, to address multiple positions of others instead of holding and defending your own views. This, too, will have an effect on how the system as a whole interacts. Paradoxically, it may lead to your own views being heard. But you will probably find that this becomes less important as you experience the capability of your "problem system" to co-create its own solutions. As this happens, you will be experiencing the meaning of the phrase, "shifting to a constructionist stance". Do it often enough, and you will achieve the shift of identity we talk about in Chapter 8, where the new behaviours become established and self-sustaining.

Maybe you find it difficult to conceive of managing to act in this way, of initiating the new pattern of relating across your system without your boss's support. A way out of this dilemma is again to look for a position that reconciles what seem as self-cancelling options. Often we find this occurs because clients cannot conceive of a position in which they are both one thing and another, contrary to the first. Systemic thinkers talk about resolving these dilemmas by taking the *both/and position*. For example, how can you be a loyal subordinate *and* act in a non-sanctioned and new way? The key is to look for areas of your role, parts of your work system within which you can act differently in doing what your unit's objectives require of you. Not everything you do in your role is completely specified by job descriptions and consciously sanctioned by your boss. Large areas are available for you to interpret. You have more space for innovation than you perhaps realize. You can trial your new solution and still meet your formal objectives. And acting in this truly empowered way, we think you can lay the foundation of a subculture in which you and others will be heard, not just on one issue, but continually.

ENACTMENT—
THE BRIDGE FROM BEING HEARD TO BEING VALUED

Perhaps it would help now to go over some of this ground again from a different perspective. In what follows we describe in some detail the sort of interaction with a client that leads to an assignment being specified that is "systemic enough".

We were invited by a Personnel Director, Marjorie, to come and discuss our type of helping, after a colleague in another company had recommended us as a group who were different and perceptive. (This is an example of the indirect route to the beginning of a conversation, the ex-client taking responsibility for "packaging" us, using mutually understood language—always better than our "foreign" words, however much care we take to express ourselves simply.)

When we first met Marjorie, she had found just the focus for making sure that the precious time given up for our meeting might not be totally wasted (another belief that creates difficulty for new consulting practices wishing to widen their range of contacts). Her Managing Director had that morning dumped a new problem on her overloaded desk. He was clearly deflecting onto her some pressures he was getting from the Product Managers (three in all, covering the new "business" product groupings). They were getting more annoyed at the behaviour of the Marketing Services Manager: a direct report to the Marketing Director, something to do with "getting people's backs up", "standing on form", "interrogating" anyone who approached him for help, rather than acting as a "colleague". The issue had actually reached as far as being raised in the Executive Committee, but the discussion got nowhere. The Managing Director was annoyed at this and had decided to act. He wanted Marjorie to take action but try to avoid dismissals and any scraps that would get them involved with an Industrial Tribunal. "What would you do?" enquired our hostess.

The first surprise for her was that we didn't seem to want to know, at the start, about the problem managers or the disputes. Instead, we tried to find out something about the Managing

Director, his position with regard to the Executive Committee members, and the possible meaning of his action and involvement of Marjorie. What might explain the way he had presented the issue? What ideas might he want to convey, and to whom, by acting in this way? Her surprise at this line of questioning allowed us to digress and explain a bit about the concept of observed and observing systems (see Chapter 2).

As we went on questioning around the problem, we were able to introduce some of our other ways of thinking. We could illustrate the social construction of the "reality" of this problem individual's behaviour as we asked about the connections between the various people who shared the same view of the Marketing Services Manager, Joe. What was the pattern of interactions that might have led to this distinction of "high-handedness" becoming widely shared? Questions about the gradual shift in people's response to Joe led to some clarification about what we meant by a problem-determined system (see Chapter 1).

Marjorie asked whether we could see any way in which the problem could be resolved by tightening up the job descriptions of both Joe and the Product Managers. Or could the reporting relationship be made clearer, with Joe being tied in more to the Product Managers, but still maintaining a functional reporting line to the Marketing Director? This led us into a differentiation of task system and role idea, and the connection between beliefs and behaviour in explaining why organizations function as they do. So even if roles and structure were refined, Joe would only behave differently if the way he understood those changes matched the new behaviour of others in the system, which would connect with their new understanding of the system and Joe's new behaviour.

Then we spent some time exploring the language of this system. "Collegiality" was an important construct. What would be the effect on the system's behaviour, we wondered, if Joe's behaviour could be recognized as also being in some way "collegiate"? This was a difficult one for Marjorie. So we asked, what did he do when he was being "not collegial"? That connected with his "being a stickler", apparently, about the setting of precise terms of reference for market research assignments, especially when they involved outside agencies and preparations for the final launch of new products. We explained the impact of the concepts of reframing and

positive connotation (see Glossary), and the way they worked by finding a different level of thinking at which the distinctions between "good" and "bad" behaviours could be reversed. In this case, we wondered if Joe *not* being a stickler, at the level of the company's performance against competitors, would represent *bad* or *non-collegial* behaviour?

This linguistic approach rather appealed to Marjorie—she liked the neat reversal of meaning. So we tried some more: "traditionalist" was another distinction we explored, to see whether there were connections with the positive form of other distinctions, for example, between his being "traditional" and his "rigorousness"—a more positive way of saying "stickler".

We also looked at the sort of distinctions that would have been made "before the problem" and since. This was more familiar territory for Marjorie. She explained that since the last wave of redundancies, when an important new product launch had gone so wrong, not only had the internal market-research department been cut back, but product managers were getting more careful about covering their backs with research. Joe held the budget for this, as the former Head of Market Research, and his budget was always hitting the ceiling as a result. It didn't help that Joe always let people know he had argued against the changes, and that he believed in-house research gave better value for money.

We felt we were close to making a difference now, and began to look for the meaning that the problem represented in the system—how it saved other managers from having to make certain decisions. As we identified some dilemmas, we were able to explain how these typically lead to problem behaviour and difficulty in finding solutions in organizations. The view that Marjorie created with our help linked two dilemmas. For the Product Managers, they wanted one aspect of Joe, approachability *and* rigour, but not "non-collegiality". The Managing Director was in a fix too. He had to make his overhead cuts stick, so could not accept budget overspends, but neither could he afford any more product flops. So he needed good market-research work, but could do without being reminded by Joe about the risk he took in getting out of his last dilemma, by cutting headcount in Marketing Services in favour of external services. Now we began to understand the way in which the Managing Director had packaged the problem he handed to

Marjorie. He could not fire Joe, because the Product Managers would then find themselves on the line for controlling the crucial market-research task.

With this "news of difference" to hand, we were able to show Marjorie how the "Joe problem" connected to a systemic dilemma. We wrote it up on the flip chart in her office: "In times of financial stringency, it makes sense to cut fixed costs and buy in specialist services as needed, but handing control of the purchase of such services to generalist managers runs the risk that standards will decline, affecting competitiveness." The company's solutions had been to retain Joe for his expertise, but have him share authority for decisions over market research while retaining full accountability—not a comfortable position. We went on to suggest that we should work with the wider system on helping them to explore a better way out of the problem that the previous solution had landed them in. Having seen how we worked, felt the effect of reframing, and understood more about the way beliefs form "problem systems", Marjorie had no difficulty agreeing to recommend our constructionist approach to the Managing Director as a cost-effective way to a different order of solution.

This is a good example of enactment in selling—involving the client in developing the "invisible fit". If clients find that this process of exploring their problem issue leads to its disappearance, without the need to implement a special action or change programme, what will they attribute to the presence and activity of the consultant/internal change agent? If solutions are simply the absence of a feeling any more that there is a problem, and arise out of what to the client appears to be a process of preliminary exploration, will they feel that there is any credit (let alone payment) that they need to give to the consultant?

GETTING TO BE VALUED— FEELING THE INVISIBLE FIT

This leads into a further problem, that of creating a fair and equitable basis for a long-term client relationship. At one level, of course, it is our aim to help the client system to a new view of their beliefs and experience in which they no longer sense they have a problem, but instead can decide fluently on their own actions. But for an on-going client relationship to be established, the client has to come to recognize the agency of the consultant in the disappearance of their problem, and to value it. Without this, there is no motivation to continue "paying away" scarce financial resources on external agents (or accept internal transfer charges for the work of in-house helpers).

The key we have found is for us to establish with the client very clear criteria that can be used for acknowledging that they have been helped with a problem, that a change has occurred that has made a difference. This is where the FORESEE® selling model (see Chapter 6) comes into its own. By questioning thoroughly about the implications of failing to solve the problem, not only does one build up the clarity of need in the client's mind, but one can also question about how, and by what means, the client will know that their problem has been solved. Equally, by including in the context-setting stage of the selling process questions about the solutions that have already been tried and their outcomes, as well as about solutions still being applied, the consultants can more clearly set out, at the closing stage of the negotiation, a relative benchmark to indicate the impact of the intervention. Anything better than the impact of previous measures is clearly an improvement.

Equally, in questioning about relationships and behaviour around the problem in the selling process, the consultant can begin to set the benchmarking of another set of criteria of intervention effectiveness. This concerns the behaviour, of self and others, that the client is able to identify as resulting from the successful resolution of the problem. If the problem no longer exists, how will the client *see* themselves behaving differently towards others, and how will others be able to respond differently to the client or among each other?

Somewhere along this path of marketing and selling conversations, the basis of a commercial relationship will be formalized (see Figure 8). But here, too, we think that the constructionist practice will evolve a different and more cooperative connection with the client organization. Our aim is to establish a long-term business relationship, but not in the sense that we think clients would usually apply to their dealings with large commercial consultancy practices.

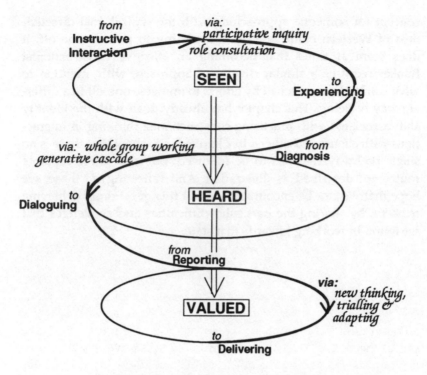

Figure 8.   **The route to acceptance**

We accept the role of catalysts of change, and know that it will take a sometimes discontinuous, complex, and drawn-out path. So our aim is to become sufficiently trusted by the client as part of their system that we can make our contributions "little and often", tracking the evolution of the client system, but not being a heavy cost burden to it. We hope to establish a perception of value that will move us away from "this assignment is the last" and towards "this is our latest chance to make a difference". We like to think that our relationship with the client is not one where we push to gain entry, but one where we respond to the client's invitation and then pull back, having made a difference that will provide the motivation for another invitation.

This resonance with T'ai Chi, the "pushing hands" exercise, makes the bridge nicely to our final chapter. The oriental disciplines stress in their different ways that "mastery" is an elusive

concept for someone approaching with the typical goal-directed-
ness of Western cultures. Without wishing to put anyone off, it
does seem at times that becoming an effective constructionist
thinker requires a similar duality of approach, with attention to
what can be done matched by efforts to immerse oneself in a different way of being. This chapter has already dealt with the identity
shift associated with practising constructionist thinking in interactions with clients and others. In Chapter 8, we show that there is no
single pathway that has to be followed; our own three separate
routes are described as illustration. And reflecting on these, we
hope that we can be encouraging about this question of achieving
mastery, by sharing the particular difficulties and challenges that
we found in working towards that state.

CHAPTER 8

Learning to take up the constructionist position

Personal reflections— experiences of the journey

What is it that makes people migrate? What is it that they see or know that impels them to undertake a long journey, putting themselves to various levels of risk and discomfort for an uncertain eventual gain? That seems to be a suitable metaphor that covers our own experience. What was it that led us to give up a comfortable and remunerative practice within an accepted community of consultants and a generally accepted framework of thinking about business management, problem resolution, and change facilitation? What was it about our particular experiences or our way of approaching the role of consultant that might have predisposed us to "mental migration"? These are questions that, at the end of this book, we thought some of our readers would be interested to hear discussed. It might help others decide whether this is a journey they can and want to undertake. It might be a useful frame for others to help them understand some of the distinctions we have been making in the earlier chapters. In the process, it might help people make their own choice to "hit the trail" in their practice as change agents, managers, or consultants.

T here is no single route or set of experiences that explains why we should have evolved in our thinking and practice in the way that we have. We can only speak as individuals. It seems to be a trail that one can pick up at various points, although, interestingly, there are not many joining points at present from the field of conventional management theory or from business school curricula.

In line with the idea of **structure-determined change** (see Glossary) from the field of biology, we are not surprised that the route to becoming a systemic thinker should be difficult to specify. People, like organisms, respond to perturbations in their environment in ways that reflect their inner structures. These structures include their mental processes, their mind-maps, which are laid down and continuously shaped by experiences. And these experiences are specific to the individual, any generality we believe we can make about these experiences being constructed by each of us in observing individuals we come across. So in this chapter we have to speak to you as individuals, leaving you to decide whether you can find a general pattern of "how to become a constructionist thinker" which makes sense to you, given your internal structures of experience.

TIM

I can think of a number of early influences that connect with the way in which I picked up the "systemic trail". At school, significant teachers in their interaction with pupils enacted their belief in the value of "bridging the disciplines" of arts and science. Equally, within that culture, innovation was valued; your personal mission was to be alert for the new. The purpose of living was the "travelling". The route was pointed out there, too: "connect, only connect" as a stance that was later reinforced by reading Koestler. As a student geologist, too, I could not ignore the idea of continual evolution, nor the individual's inevitable involvement in this "ontogeny recapitulating phylogeny".

From then on, I am aware that I have always been irked by having to remain within the bounds of a particular discipline. At university, as an economist and student of politics, I found my way into lectures on soil formation in the department of agricultural chemistry, on "problems of mind" in the philosophy department, and ethnology in the geography department. At work, as a planner in the oil industry, it was the same—getting involved in developing a new approach to forecasting, substituting conventional trend-projection techniques with analysis of the technological and economic "drivers" of structural change in markets. As a management consultant too, my story is about repeated evolution, the "ontogeny" of my own development bound up with the "phylogeny" of the changes in the role and techniques of the management consultancy profession.

I am aware that, since 1970, when I first became a management consultant, the profession has evolved considerably, although earlier species still roam the corporate marketplace. From functional expert in marketing and planning, through management structure and systems specialist, through to performance improver, my own development then took me into the area of organization culture, advising on the implementation of strategy through changing the values, norms, and behaviours of whole groups of people, whether within one firm or in a merger between companies. The drive through all my transitions has been to find more effective means by which I could help organizations achieve improved performance.

Throughout this evolution, a standard theme recurred—resistance. At first it showed itself in the common form of the consultant's expert report being used as a doorstop or otherwise devalued by non-use, the expert content (or the presentation?) presumably unacceptable to the client. At other times, clients failed to operate system designs in the way the consultant intended. As the scope of work moved ambitiously to culture change, the issue of resistance could not be ignored. But neither could I accept that it was inevitable, as many colleagues seemed to argue. There was something about the interaction between consultant and client system that felt wrong. I began to search for a different explanation, and for a different mode of consulting that would be more congenial.

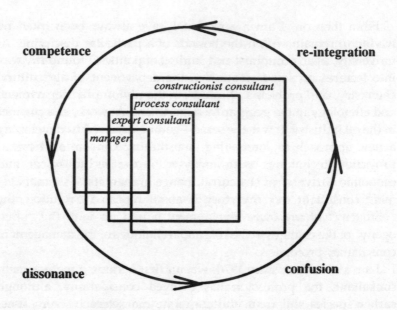

Figure 9. **The migrant's progress:**
from manager to constructionist consultant

The special, random trigger of my own evolution came from my wife, who, after completing a psychology degree, became a marriage counsellor. Her training "infected" the household with tracts on therapy, which I picked up. Resistance I could now characterize as a "defence mechanism", and it was even possible to think of organizations falling into different classes of "neurotic dysfunction". Through NTL and The Tavistock Institute, **Rogerian** and **psychodynamic** frames of thinking (see Glossary) began to influence management thinking. But although working with the Tavistock people showed me how it was possible to operationalize this frame of thinking in working with clients, I was also aware of its "bruising" effect. Sometimes it seemed a very blunt instrument for the purpose, and too imprecise in its effect to be marketable to the sort of large corporate clients with whom I was used to dealing.

Now the pace of evolution really began to quicken. Group psychodynamics begat an interest in group therapy, which led quickly to **structural** and **strategic** family therapies (see Glossary).

This was where my own story began to leave the experience and ways of thinking of the business and consultancy communities.

It was at this point, I am now aware, that a particular difference in my behaviour first occurred that was to become a key to my future ability to evolve into a constructionist thinker. It involved deliberately taking a step into a different area of work, meeting the people who inhabited the world of family therapy, and ultimately actually living partly in that world at the same time as I continued to work in business consultancy. I was introduced to the work of the Milan Centre team (Palazzoli, Boscolo, Cecchin, & Prata, 1978), and to articles from the journal *Family Process* on the *circular interviewing* technique of the Milan Group.

My development now took a spiralling form: from reading to meeting new people to new experiences back to further reading. I met my colleague Keith Kinsella, and only after some time did I find that he had arrived, via a different route, at the same conclusion as I had about the usefulness of systemic thinking in business management and consultancy. So maybe this is the place to find out about Keith's path of migration.

KEITH

My first steps along the constructionist path started towards the end of my civil engineering training, when I was particularly attracted to the "structural" end of the discipline. Identifying the forces that might act on the structure, working out the resulting distribution of stresses across members, was always a challenging and complex task. Later in the mid-1960s, when I moved into the construction end of the business, I found that the new approaches to project control using network methods of PERT and Critical Path Analysis held a similar fascination.

Looking back, I now realize that what interested me was the way these methods could apparently capture *whole systems*, by mapping the important connections and information on interaction patterns. At the time, I think I saw these models as close representations of the "reality" of the structures and projects they described, but very much as closed systems. Now I see that they can also be understood as mental constructions, which nevertheless can be

experienced as both constraining and enabling, just like their concrete and steel counterparts.

During a three-year stay in Ontario, my awareness developed of
the social and psychological aspects of systems. Work study training and the organization behaviour theories of March and Simon,
which I had studied during a year at Edinburgh University, helped
as I carried out a wide range of studies on the construction management of a large power station. What started off as a technical
study soon became embroiled in the inter-group dynamics between
the three main functional groups in the management team. It became clear that the "softer" aspects of the system usually had more
impact on performance than the technical side. Change, too, was
not like a critical path network, but much more a loosely linked
evolutionary process. During the next five years in general management, I became more aware of how poorly the conventional
theories on human and organization behaviour worked in practice.

During a first spell of consultancy, I can now see that I operated
very much from the first-level cybernetic position, that if you were
clever enough, you could understand complex systems and make
proposals to solve problems. The concept of "bounded rationality"
explained why clients did not implement these ideas as intended—
that is, resisted the changes proposed. My rather blinkered
"structural" and strongly logical approach was opened up by two
things: my increasing interest in the socio-technical insights of
Emery and Trist (1960), and a boss who pursued an almost wholly
intuitive and personal "influence the Chief Executive" approach.
Between socio-technical theory and his interpersonal practice, I
began to realize how important the psychology of the individual
and the dynamics of groups were for effective change in organizations.

In 1979, when I left the Human Resources development consultancy to join the Grubb Institute, I had reached the stage
where I felt ignorant of what made individuals and organizations
tick. I also realized that I was much more interested in looking
at things that cut across the usual functional boundaries, and that
I disliked a short-term operational emphasis. At the Grubb, I had
my introduction to the Tavistock model of consulting, with its
hypothesizing about the impact of "unconscious" processes in
group interactions. But the most fundamental experience was a

fortuitous involvement with Irving Borwick on an assignment with ITT. He introduced me to the ideas of the Milan Family Therapy Centre, and to the work he, Cecchin, Boscolo, and Bruce Reed of the Grubb Institute were carrying out to apply these ideas in organizations. While it was another decade before I actively took on this challenge myself, that initial connection took me actively into exploring a whole new world in which, like Tim, I was a beginner. Much "personal" time was spent in trying to understand the concepts, models, and methods of this rapidly developing "school" of systemic thinking, as I went about my daily work in a more conventional way.

During a busy working life as Head of Personnel with a multi-national surface coatings supplier, three particularly influential approaches crossed my path:

1. Neurolinguistic programming (NLP: Sinclair, 1992) and Ericksonian methods (O'Hanlon, 1987) made me more aware of the importance of language in how we represent our experience, and the powerful impact of presuppositions in limiting or empowering our views of what is possible.

2. "Soft systems methodology" (Checkland, 1981) introduced a way of visually representing cognitive processes and how context could influence people's ideas of purpose and what had to be done to effect improvements.

3. The use of a conversational approach (Reason & Rowan, 1981) in helping people get in touch with the real issues facing them, particularly where cultural changes were required.

My interest in culture change then took me to another consultancy, where I met Tim. Having exchanged thoughts on our dissatisfactions with current consulting practices, we both joined in pursuing our shared interest in the systemic thinking that was being developed by family therapists and others interested in the methods being developed in that field. Training and conversations with leading practitioners brought home to us a conviction that we needed a new context in which to develop what we both felt was the way ahead for effective consulting and organization change.

The next step again involved the risk of trying new experience. Tim and I left to form our own consultancy, aiming to develop as

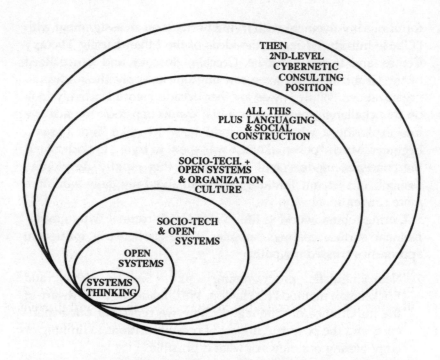

Figure 10. **Another migrant's map:
developments in conceptual thinking**

systemic thinkers by trying to apply what we were learning to our work as consultants in business (see Chapters 2 and 6). We now introduced ourselves to David Campbell and Ros Draper, who were practising as family therapists at the Tavistock Clinic and providing occasional consultations to organizations as well as writing an excellent series of books and articles on the Milan systemic model of family therapy and consultation. We continued with them the cycle of reading, practising, and putting ourselves through new and unfamiliar experiences.

DAVID

My story begins in Boston, Massachusetts, where I completed a Ph.D. programme in clinical psychology in 1971. Although the emphasis of this training was on psychotherapy, I was also exposed to a form of systemic thinking through the pioneering work of Gerald Caplan, who advocated that preventative work should be done by professionals getting into the community, understanding how the community-based structures work, and stimulating change from the grass-roots level upwards. Over the years since my training, I have always done some work as a consultant to teams and small organizations, but largely on the basis of the "psychology" of group dynamics and staff development problems. However, it is only recently that I feel I have acquired the conceptual tools to enable me to do effective work within larger organizations.

I had worked for many years with individuals and couples in clinical settings, but in the late 1970s I was beckoned by a new area of work known as family therapy. My attraction to working with family groups seemed based on the excitement of being in the midst of a living, interacting group of people. I also liked the way in which I could see the tangible results of my work. I had the illusion that I could crack the mystery of family life and discover "how families worked" because relationships would be played out in front of my eyes. A family is solid, but also plastic, which means that a therapist can often see the result of his interventions through the changes in the behaviour of individual family members. The family was a team, a unit, a system, and I have always been fascinated by the way individuals can work together to make something greater than the sum of themselves. Early thinking in this field focused on structural properties of family life such as the alliances and boundaries amongst members, and the therapist frequently held a template in his mind of the way a family structure should be in order to function well.

In the late 1970s a new approach to family treatment was devised by a group in Milan (Palazzoli et al., 1970) which was awarded the label "systemic family therapy". This shifted the emphasis from the smaller family unit to the family in its larger ecology; and from analysing structures to understanding the meaning system that guides behaviour. The concept of second-order cybernetics, which put the observer squarely in the system he was observing, was an exciting part of this new package. The Milan group also clarified a number of techniques that became essential tools in my own practice: the injunction to organize one's thinking at the outset in the form of a "systemic hypothesis"; the practice of asking "circular questions", which attempt to connect bits of information to the larger pattern; and the attempt on the part of the consultant to retain a neutral position and not to be drawn to one point of view at the expense of others.

Working at the Tavistock Clinic, which is a large NHS post-qualification training centre, I soon became a supervisor of other family therapists. For some of the time, I sat behind an observation mirror supervising other therapists' work with families. I had to step back and put myself in the position of consultant to the system of therapist-and-family that was being created on the other side of the screen. In order to make effective suggestions for the therapist I had to observe the way the therapist and the family members were influencing each other.

Most of the professionals who came to the Clinic for training faced problems when they tried to put new ideas into practice in their own workplace, and, as a result, I also turned my attention to understanding the position of the trainees in their own agency. I was forced to think about the organizational effects of someone coming back from a course and trying to introduce change. Most of the trainees failed until we began to understand this as a systemic process, and to design more appropriate ways for trainees to introduce change.

I soon realized that the same conceptual tools I had applied to families could be applied to organizations. I found that people within organizations naturally understood that departments and functions interacted, but because they were a part of the organization themselves, they could not step back and see this process. It proved helpful, and at times liberating, for people to understand that their behaviour could be seen in a completely different context when one looked at the influences from other parts of the system.

But I discovered that conceptualizing about an organization is one thing and working as a consultant is another! The latter required a range of skills to do with understanding primary tasks, mission statements, communication patterns, and strategic thinking, all of which I was only beginning to learn. This is why I was very interested in that first phone call from Keith. He described his work and his partnership with Tim, and it seemed that each of us

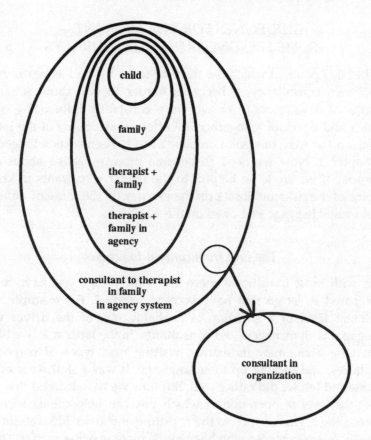

Figure 11.   **The migration of therapist to consultant**

(along with Ros Draper, who joined us at the beginning) could contribute something distinctive to a new venture which became the development of something new: a constructionist approach to consultation.

The partnership has enabled us to transform systemic ideas into a consistent practice; to adapt public sector work to the private sector, and vice versa; and to present ourselves as a consultancy service, which has meant carefully defining our relationship with the clients, and finding ways to explain our work which are both intelligible and compelling.

GUIDELINES FOR THE MIGRANT—
SOME LESSONS FROM OUR JOURNEYS

After this point, at which the three of us had joined as partners in our own consultancy, it becomes harder to talk about separate paths of development, for we were constantly influencing each other and developing together in various ways. Some of the influences on us from this point on have already been acknowledged in Chapter 2. Now we need to become more reflective about our journey if we are to be helpful to the reader who wants to know some of the risks and losses on the journey (in the sense of unhelpful mental baggage jettisoned on the way).

The shift from content to process

As with most transitions, there are some things you have to be prepared to let go that have become habitual. For example, the content level of a situation is probably one of the drives that engages both managers and consultants. In the latter role, we liked learning about new industries, visiting new types of corporate cultures, and picking up their language. It was a skill we used to hone and felt we did rather well. But now we have learned that it is not the level of operation at which you can help clients without becoming "symmetrical" to them, pitting one's own ideas about the business against those who have much more experience of it. There is a different sort of content, what Keeney (1983) calls "politics", to which we had to become attuned.

This "politics" is the pattern of "concrete", inter-connected happenings, the actions resulting from beliefs held which link different parts of a system and provide feedback to either confirm or challenge those beliefs. It represents a level of thinking with which most clients are not familiar. Our cultural formation inclines us all to a more linear outlook, of causes and points of blame or dysfunction. As it is a part of our reflexes, too, we have to work hard at countering it so that we can offer our clients a different perspective, based on an awareness of circular patterns of causation. This level of "content" does not lead to our being symmetrical to the client in terms of challenging their knowledge of their business, their expertise. However, it is symmetrical to their expectation of what consultants and problem solvers should pay attention to. So the would-be constructionist consultant/manager has to overcome a double pressure: from his own "cultural training" as well as from the client's expectations of helpful behaviour.

The shift from expert to co-creator

Connected with this shift from content, we had to learn, in preparing for meetings with the client, to take our efforts at briefing ourselves a stage further. This level of content had to be used to build a hypothesis about the way in which the problematic issue might be connecting the interests of different parts of the client system in either changing or not changing (see the section on "Influencing the Hierarchy" in Chapter 7).

As we made this shift away from content, we found we had to leave behind two further reflexes that consulting practice had "structured" into us. One was the joy of "being right", being "cleverer" than the client, and so being the source of change in the client's policies or procedures. A related reflex was of predicting something the client system was not aware of, by making wider connections, grasping the influence of more variables in a complex system. As a constructionist consultant, you have to learn how to see the "rightness" in any client position, and how to help clients be curious about the positions that others, including yourselves, feel could equally be "right". You also need to stay curious yourself about how these different views might be connected by a different framing of the context in which they are set. From predicting, you have to move to be equally interested in "re-storying": how a client might see a way they could make different distinctions about their situation that would leave them free to begin to create a different sort of future, free from the problematic issue. The thrill now has to be vicarious, sharing the client's satisfaction in being able to make their own different "prediction" for their future.

And in describing that shift, we are aware that we are beginning to express the essence of the shift in consulting style that we had been looking for in the latter years of our practice. It has been a shift from the logical and analytical generalization or abstraction from experience towards working in the narrative mode, using the local experiences of people. There is a further shift within this transition, however.

The shift from control to appreciation

All the time we have had to be aware of the ways in which the client may be trying (unconsciously) to "organize" our responses to fit with their preferred way of looking at things, knowing that if we fall in with it, we are not going to be able to be as helpful as if we counter the invitation. We have to learn *not* to settle for the story the client wants to tell, but to realize that it is just one view of a larger, richer picture. So we have always to remain curious about the meaning behind our client wanting to tell us their story in their particular way. And this involves a completely different stance from the expert consultant. You have to remind yourself that you *don't* know what the client means when they use constructs, so that you can ask , "What does someone *do* when they are being (whatever it is)"; this is the route to the content of "politics" in the client system. Instead of trying to be "one up" in the relationship with the client, you have to learn to be comfortable with being "one down"—"No, I don't know what you mean; can you tell me how you know that?"

Connected with this "one-down" stance is learning to love "being wrong". By this we mean *not* minding when the questions you construct, based on a steadily growing conviction that your hypothesis really explains this client system, produce information that does not fit. You have to learn to want just this sort of feedback, because it enables you to remake your hypothesis in a richer form that will suggest a new line of questioning that will probably lead to greater understanding, by you as well as the client, of the meaning of their problem in that system.

This search for feedback to enrich your hypothesis helps you maintain a productive working relationship with the client system, and to counter the tendency we have noticed for our socialization to lead us to avoid difference. For example, it is so easy to drop into answering a direct question from the client about "What would you do in this situation?" All one's social reflexes suggest that it is discourteous not to respond to another's questions. But the more useful response is to be able to ask the client a question in return that may help to reveal a new meaning to the distinction that lay behind their question. For example, where you are talking to one manager who feels a colleague is being "political" and competitive in his response to proposals for change, instead of suggesting a course of action, you have to ask something like: "What might this other manager be trying to show you about your change ideas that is positive for the company when looked at from his perspective? What does this enable him to do, and what does it mean he can avoid doing?" The benefit of your hypothesizing is that it enables you always to be deciding whether providing what your client (and social mores) expects from the relationship will be useful in introducing difference from which they can learn, or whether acting counter to their expectations might be more productive.

The shift to irreverence

As was touched on in Chapter 7, clients have a particular view about the way that consulting help should be provided. In management development, for example, they expect to be talked to about ideas and cases, and to be given hand-outs that summarize all this. As consultants, we have had to work very hard to find ways of allowing the client to be "right" about all this, and yet, when appropriate, to act also in ways that we guess may be more effective in achieving real learning. For example, in talking about ideas, we might try to find a way of presenting their complementary aspects, as in the pairing of "leadership" requirements of a strategy with the "managership" aspects. In talking about cases, we might choose to balance external examples with a form of feedback to the client which helps them to see aspects of their own company as equally worthy of being "a case". In helping clients with problem solving, we have had to restrain our earlier reflexes to follow the client into "hunting the solution". Instead, we find it is more helpful to hold back, to "keep them in the sweat box", exploring the meaning of the problem in the client system so thoroughly that the underlying dilemma eventually surfaces. Then we find that they are better positioned to evolve a solution that strikes a balance, is "right enough" for the moment.

Clients also have clear ideas about the reason they are calling on consultants for help, and on what they want as the outcome from an assignment. All the guidelines managers are given about "managing consultants" tell them that if they do not have this sorted out in their minds, they will end up with an unsatisfactory assignment. Again, it is difficult for the new constructionist practitioner to avoid falling in with this. What is more helpful, we have now realized, is to start with questioning that implicitly challenges this clarity in the client's mind. We need to explore the meaning of this person, at this time, involving this consultancy, in this particular formulation of the problem. Who else is connected to the nominal client? What is the meaning of change for these others and the nominal client? We do this because we have found that as well as being informative for the client, it establishes something very important for our assignment—a degree of space and freedom to do the unconventional/unexpected, because the client now has an experience of its usefulness.

The shift from comfort to exploration

Finally, we need to throw some light on the process of one's self-development as a constructionist practitioner. For example, one aspect of the journey now strikes us. It seems to have been very important always to take the risk of putting ourselves just beyond the level of comfort, of certain competence in all these new situations. The result has often been confusion and personal embarrassment. Turning points in understanding of systemic concepts seem to be reached via a discussion that initially leaves you confused, as you let go of long-held views. Re-reading relevant articles, followed by personal experimentation and further discussion, are needed before you realize that now you understand something additional to what before you thought was the essence of an argument.

You have to work very hard at making your mind work more flexibly, at breaking away from your usual way of thinking. You especially need to work on the new skill of finding different "framings", settings within which a story can mean something different to the client, and less problem-filled. You need to become fluent at using the techniques for revealing useful differences in meanings behind actions—to yourself and to the client. You need to work at this, because above all you need to be able to relate to clients flexibly and naturally. Your use of techniques has to become subconscious, so that they do not intrude on your connectedness to the client system.

This is something to be approached constantly. The journey is a long one, and done by *living* the new approach. It is best to pace one's development, becoming consistent in one aspect of this way of thinking so that it properly informs your practice before you move on and try refinements. When there are so many channels that make up the mainstream flow of systemic thinking, it can be tempting to divert down an interesting tributary suggested by a colleague. The risk is that your working with clients becomes confused, as you become too conscious of applying a new variant of the thinking, so that you lose the positive feedback of seeing clarity emerge in the client system. And when you fear you are getting stuck through your experimenting, it is useful to have that platform of consistency to return to, to help you re-connect with the client. Simple questions to yourself can help, such as wondering what it is that you are feeling you ought *not* to do, and thinking of the effect on the client if you were to do it; or becoming aware of the idea you have that you are not daring to challenge, and setting about asking the questions that will test that idea. These moves help remind you that you are a participant-observer in the system, helping to construct the sense of the problem. Your connection to the client system will be restored.

We are aware how hard it is to "get inside" the constructionist way of thinking without some live training and then supervised practice. To avoid the trap of applying this approach at the level of technique, one needs an informed observer to challenge one to think about implications and of connections, particularly of one's own connection to the client system's functioning. So the would-be migrant would do well to find a supportive group with which to make the journey. At present, this support network of peers probably does not exist widely outside the therapy community. We have been fortunate in our development that this community has been built around a belief in the value of sharing new thinking and appreciating difference. This has allowed us to draw continuing inspiration from developments in that field without needing to choose between living either as family therapists or as management consultants. Our intention (see Postscript) connected with the writing of this book is to widen this idea of a practising community to include people from the different worlds of industry, government, public service, education, and the caring professions. We hope to create a forum where these very different experiences are valued and from which everyone can draw support in developing constructionist thinking skills and building a different practitioner-identity. Systemic thinking makes us well aware, too, of the effect that starting on this journey can have on the system of relationships in the manager's own workplace (see also Guy's position in the case in Chapter 4). It can be especially helpful to be able to discuss these reactions from the rest of the system to one's changing with others who share your new way of thinking; not in terms of simple support, but more in thinking through one's own part in the development of those problematic reactions.

RETROSPECT AND PROSPECT

Looking back now with the systemic perspective more firmly in place, it has been possible to "reconstruct" the story of our past consulting work and view it as more of a continuum. This, too, may be reassuring for the would-be migrant. Not everything of one's old thinking has to be left behind. There were aspects of our work that we can now see had the seeds of a systemic approach in them.

For example, in the latter years there was much more emphasis on thinking about the organization as a complete system, where beliefs were linked to current action, and where problems of resistance to change were seen as people doing their best to continue acting in what they saw as the best interests of the organization. What was missing was the non-directive way of operating on these beliefs to bring organization and people into alignment. Instead, the emphasis was on radical structure change and the replacement of key people as a means of "infecting" the culture with change agents to trigger the adaptation of the wider system.

The social construction of meaning was there, in embryo, in the emphasis on working to create consensus about a feasible route for change. The trouble was that the dialogue was restricted to the leadership group, and the process gave way to "instructive communication" thereafter for the rest of the organization.

Standing back from our transition, we are aware that one constant struggle through all this has been to achieve the position where one *is* a systemic thinker in a situation rather than is trying to respond in a systemic way. Keeney (1983) has put it well with his analogy of mastering the art of Zen archery. The more one is trying to hit the target, the Zen master tells the student, the further one gets from mastering the art. It seems like making the transition from consciously attempting to be unconscious in one's practice of systemic thinking to being unconsciously conscious in one's work.

And if you want to know where the journey ends, or where we are headed next, the answer has to be that one must continually try to master the art of constructionist thinking by practice. There is no end. To ask whether one has mastered the art is probably to admit that one has not.

Next steps

*Moving from knowledge to experience
as a basis for enactment*

What can readers do who have been caught by the ideas in this book and who can understand intellectually the distinctiveness of this approach, but who rightly want to try out its application in a safe environment before attempting to introduce it in their own company or practice? What route forward is there for the internal change agent who is looking for new insights that will give an edge in tackling organizational problems, but who needs the reassurance of seeing these ideas applied in practice before recommending their wider use in the organization?

King's Consulting Partners is the development business operated by the authors. We offer a programme of "open courses" to bridge this gap between knowledge and experience. These are focused on themes of current interest, as well as introducing the basics of systemic thinking. They offer the possibility of applying this thinking to participants' current work issues around each course subject. Their focus is on improving managers' abilities to deliver practical results in their work context.

The range of these courses currently comprises:

- **Introduction to Constructionist Consulting**

  Three modules, each of two days' duration, which deal with the key concepts, approach, and methods of the constructionist approach to consulting. Particularly suitable for practising consultants or internal change agents.

- **Managing System Change**

  A three-day workshop introducing the systemic approach to change management, which can be used by internal change agents to identify new options for working with resistance during change programmes.

- **Managing for Results**

  A five-day course on systemic project management, which helps lay the foundations for more consistent delivery of results from projects that require people to change.

Other programmes are provided for in-house organizational and management development, covering the following themes:

Empowering Individuals: Courses about enabling individual growth, creating two-way communications, and improving role effectiveness.

Enhancing Teamwork: Courses that establish contexts for effective participation, team self-management, and using team diversity.

Developing Organization Capabilities: Courses about managing strategically at the local level, dis-solving problems, and information resourcing.

Course venues and frequencies are varied to match demand. For further information please contact:

The Course Administrator, King's Consulting Partners, King's College London, Campden Hill Road, Kensington, London W8 7AH.

GLOSSARY

analogic: a non-verbal means of communicating, using physical movements and expressive bodily actions, including speech tone and volume variations. There is often a close equivalence between the content of what is being communicated and the choice of these means. For example, irritation might be expressed by a "clipped" intonation, the lips compressed without a smile.

circularity: the situation where what happens is in some way both determined by some precursor event and has also had some effect on that first event, where it is not possible to determine "which came first, the chicken or the egg". This way of viewing the world grew out of biology and ecology. It is consistent with a *linear conception* if the latter is seen as treating just one small segment of a larger inter-related whole.

circular questioning: questions asked with the intention of revealing differences between people who are members of some system. The questioner expects that the answer will help him to refine his **working hypothesis** (see below) and so to become interested in asking a further question based on feedback from his respondent. It is this process between the questioner and the

189

respondent, driven by feedback, which changes the respondent's perspective on his situation and stimulates new thinking.

co-construction: a form of interaction between two individuals/ groups where neither preconceives the form that the output from their interaction will take, but each puts forward their respective contributions, confident that the result will be more effective than a similar effort being made by either of them alone (see also **hermeneutic**).

complementarity: a form of relationship where two people/ groups, although differing in characteristics or attributes, find that they can fit together in achieving a shared goal, either by accepting reciprocity (as in a hierarchical, one-up/one-down fit), or by the periodic and accepted reversal/alteration of their relative position.

conversational triplet: a description of the three steps required for an effective communicational episode, comprising: first, A's utterance; second, B's response linked to that utterance; and third, A's further utterance that reflects the effect that B's response has had on A's original distinctions put forward to B.

discourse: conveys the important idea (after Wittgenstein) that our concepts, the basis of our thinking, are expressed by words, which are located in language. We use these to engage in *action* with others to accomplish practical, ceremonial, and communicative activities. We can talk therefore of the *speech-act* as central to our interactions with others. This constitutes a form of life or reality in which a person can be seen as a meeting point of many discourses, i.e. a *discursive subject*.

dissipative structures: new forms of organization that arise spontaneously when systems are pushed by environmental events beyond the equilibrium point at which they can retain their previous form of organization by *first-order* or adaptive change. The re-organization is achieved by means of positive feedback loops in the system (see Chapter 1).

dualist: the *paradigmatic* position in which reality is held to exist independent of the observer, and where objectivity in the study and description of another person, group, or phenomenon is held to be possible.

ecology of ideas: the collection of individuals' beliefs—usually implicit or unconscious—that, by their inter-connectedness and mutual relevance, underpin a social system.

epistemology: the study of how we think and arrive at decisions. How we explain how we know what we know.

equifinality: a law of system relationships, which holds that the same eventual goal can be reached from differing starting points and by differing intervening processes/steps.

first-level cybernetics: this contrasts the idea of the "black box", which can have a purpose attributed to it by an outside observer by interpreting the function of feedback (first level), with situations where the attribution of the outsider becomes a *part* of the system—i.e. the system in focus is the black box plus observer (second level).

hermeneutic: interpretative (as of texts), but used also to refer to the process by which meaning and understanding are recognized as evolving in dialogue between people, where each brings his own expectations and preconceptions but allows these to be affected by contact with the meanings that the others draw from their experiences.

instructive interaction: an episode between people where the intent and belief of one person is that knowledge/beliefs that they hold can be transmitted to the other so that they will end up being able to use this knowledge/belief in precisely the way intended by the "instructor". This form of "teaching" contrasts with experiential learning types of interaction, where the objective of one person is to facilitate the development of the other's capacity for gaining new insights.

languaging: one way in which it is possible to explain how social constructions or "realities" such as problems come to exist by people sharing and agreeing about a distinction, encapsulated in words.

linear conception (linearity, linear thinking): a way of viewing/explaining events where no feedback is recognized from the effect to what is held as its cause, so that all of the effect is explained by the action of the causative agent. The essence of this way of thinking is the view of each party to an interaction as having a separate existence, and where they are not seen as in any way linked to each other as a system. (See **circularity** for the contrasting position.)

meta: (as in "taking up a meta-position") taking a view of an issue from a different, usually higher, level—e.g. metaphysics.

mind-maps: the internalized sense of the connectedness of experiences that an individual has built up through interactions with others that gives security in making decisions about action or in making sense of new experiences.

modernist: the belief that it is possible, by objective and "scientific" research, to arrive at general, universally applicable explanations of "how things work", at theories and quantifiable "models" of phenomena that can be used to predict and control events, from the way plants grow to the way people behave. (See also **universal solutions** and **dualist.**)

multiple realities: the perspective that results when reality is viewed as being created by social interaction, so that in principle "there are as many universes as there are willing describers" (Watzlawick, 1976).

negative connotation: the opposite of **positive connotation** (see below) where the explanation for a situation emphasizes a harmful or destructive effect or intent.

neutrality: a stance maintained by a helper or manager of showing equal interest in the beliefs and explanations of each party in a dispute or confrontation, reflecting in constructionist thinking the awareness of **multiple realities** (see above). The stance alone can lead to a significant shift in behaviour among system members who have only been used to privileging one construction of a situation in their attempts to solve a problem.

paradigm: a widely shared way of viewing and explaining "how things work around here" for a given community that is largely unspoken and resistant to challenge. (See also **mind-maps.**)

positive connotation/frame: a form of **reframing** (see below) in which behaviour/situations that are experienced negatively by an individual/manager are explained in ways that suggest a positive intention for the system as a whole in the behaviours of the other people/groups associated with the problem. (See also **negative connotation**.)

positivist: (as in logical positivism) a point of view that puts forward scientific observations as the only basis for assessing "truth", and that considers arguments not based on observable data as meaningless. (See also **modernist** and **dualist**.)

praxis: most simply translated as personal theory-in-action or the practical living out of one's central ideas, conditioned by a **hermeneutic** (see above) approach to understanding and developing this form of knowledge.

psychodynamic: the practice of psychotherapy, based on the theories of Freud, where the benefit for the client is held to derive from the giving of "insights" by the therapist, and the use of this insight by the client to come to different understandings of relationships, including those cases where what happens between the therapist and the client is interpreted by the therapist as repeating a pattern between the client and some significant person in their past.

punctuation: the act of choosing the point of view from which one will explain a complex set of inter-related events, as in describing to a listener the reasons for a bad relationship by starting with the actions of one of the parties.

reductionist: the belief in a method for understanding how complex systems work by breaking their operation down into small subprocesses, each of which is affected by relatively few major variables, making the measurement and prediction of outcomes more manageable. (See also **dualist**.)

reflexivity: where some action, statement, or question "turns back on itself" and leads to some change in the state of the initiating system component. Used, for example, in the context of "reflexive questions" where a helper, by asking a particular question that refers to concepts/meanings held by the client system, intends to influence the client to reorganize their understanding of those concepts in such a way that the issue no longer exists or is seen in a different light.

reframing: putting forward an alternative explanation about a situation perceived as problematic by another individual/

manager, who is unable otherwise to find any way of viewing the situation that is not problematic.

Rogerian: a form of psychotherapy developed by Carl Rogers, where the chief benefit is held to derive from the therapist showing unconditional positive regard for the client, and which encourages the free expression of feelings associated with the problem incidents and relationships.

second-level cybernetics: see **first-level cybernetics.**

strategic therapy: where the therapist negotiates goals with the family and then devises tasks for the family members to perform, the process making it difficult for them to continue with what have been diagnosed as "non-normal" behaviours. It may also help the family to achieve a transition in its evolution which had previously been blocked.

structure-determined change: derived from biology, this view proposes that the form that change takes in a system is determined by the laid-down structures of that system. In the case of human social systems, the change is linked to the prevailing beliefs and sense of context that each person has arrived at as a result of their earlier social interactions, and which are used by the individual/group as a basis for deciding on action in response to perturbations of their system.

structural therapy: where the problems experienced by a family or other system are held to be related to some deficiency in structuring their relationships (such as unclear or absent intergenerational or role boundaries). The therapist/consultant acts as a member of the system in an interaction to block/disrupt what are seen as unhelpful inter-relationships, so that by experiencing themselves in a more "normal" relationship with others, people behave differently, and the problem they previously experienced disappears.

symmetrical: (as in a symmetrical relationship) where people interact with each other in ways, usually unconscious, that lead them to feel challenged in their sense of being "on top", so leading to escalating interchanges in which each attempts to reassert this advantage over the other.

systemic hypothesis: see **working hypothesis.**

universal solutions: ideas put forward that are held to provide a generally applicable answer to a frequently occurring problem, or a means of approaching a particular task which, if followed, will always lead to successful accomplishment. These ideas derive typically from a **modernist, positivist,** and **dualist** set of beliefs.

working hypothesis: the ideas that a consultant draws together from initial contacts with the problem system concerning what may lie behind the difficulties being presented. These ideas are only meant to guide the consultant's initial questioning or research, to surface more information about distinctions held by members of the problem system. With this new information, the consultant revises the hypothesis or forms a new one, to continue the process. The aim is to arrive eventually at a *systemic hypothesis* that connects the behaviour of all the members of the system, from their particular views of the context. This systemic hypothesis can then be the basis for an intervention.

REFERENCES

Andersen, T. (1990). *The Reflecting Team*. New York: W.W. Norton.

Anderson, H., & Goolishian, H. (1988). Human systems as linguistic systems: preliminary and evolving ideas about the implications for clinical theory. *Family Process, 27* (4): 371–384.

Anderson, H., Goolishian, H., & Winderman, L. (1986). Problem-determined systems: towards transformation in family therapy. *Journal of Strategic and Systemic Therapies, 5*: 1–13.

Argyris, C. (1990). *Overcoming Organizational Defenses*. London: Allyn & Bacon.

Ashby, W. R. (1958a). General Systems Theory as a new discipline. *General Systems, 3*: 1–6.

Ashby, W. R. (1958b). *An Introduction to Cybernetics*. New York: Wiley.

Bateson, G. (1973). *Steps to an Ecology of Mind*. London: Paladin.

Beishon, J., & Peters, G. (1972). *Systems Behaviour*. London: Harper & Row.

Bernstein, R.J. (1983). *Beyond Objectivism and Subjectivism*. Oxford: Blackwell.

Block, P. (1981). *Flawless Consulting*. San Diego, CA: University Associates.

Campbell, D., Draper, R., & Huffington, C. (1991a). *A Systemic Approach to Consultation*. London: Karnac Books.

Campbell, D., Draper, R., & Huffington, C. (1991b). *Teaching Systemic Thinking*. London: Karnac Books.

Cave, E., & McKeown, P. (1993). Managerial effectiveness: the identification of need. *Management Education & Development, 24* (2).

Cecchin, G., Lane, G., & Ray, W. L. (1992). *Irreverence: A Strategy for Therapists' Survival*. London: Karnac Books.

Checkland, P. (1981). *Systems Thinking, Systems Practice*. Chichester: John Wiley.

Cronen, V., Pearce, W. B., & Tomm, K. (1985). A dialectical view of personal change. In: K. Gergen & K. Davis (Eds.), *The Social Construction of the Person*. New York: Springer-Verlag.

Deming, W. E. (1982). *Quality, Productivity and Competitive Position*. Cambridge, MA: MIT Press.

Dilts, R. B., Epstein T., & Dilts, R. W. (1991). *Tools for Dreamers*. Cupertino, CA: Meta Publications.

Emery, F. E. (1969). *System Thinking*. London: Penguin.

Emery, F. E., & Trist, E. L. (1960). Socio-technical systems. In: C. W. Churchman & M. Verhuist (Eds.), *Management Sciences, Models and Techniques*. London: Pergamon.

Garfinkel, H. (1967). *Studies in Ethnomethodology*. Cambridge: Polity Press.

Geneen, H. S. (1985). *Managing*. London: Grafton.

Gergen, K. (1985). The social constructionist movement in modern psychology. *American Psychologist*, 40: 266–275.

Gergen, K. (1992). *Remarks at the KCC Summer Conference. The Art of Systemic Management*.

Guba, E. G., & Lincoln, Y. S. (1989). *Fourth Generation Evaluation*. Newbury, CA: Sage.

Harré, R., & Gillett, G. (1994). *The Discursive Mind*. Newbury, CA: Sage.

Hampden-Turner, C. (1990). *Charting the Corporate Mind*. Oxford: Blackwell.

Hay, J. (1990). Managerial competences or managerial characteristics. *Management Education & Development, 21* (4).

Katz, D., & Kahn, R. (1966). *The Social Psychology of Organizations*. New York: John Wiley.

Keeney, B. P. (1983). *Aesthetics of Change*. New York: Guilford Press.

Lackoff, G., & Johnson, M. (1980). *Metaphors We Live By*. Chicago, IL: University of Chicago Press.

Lincoln, Y. S., & Guba, E. G. (1985). *Naturalistic Inquiry*. Newbury, CA: Sage.

Lippitt, R. (1983). Future before you plan. In: *NTL Managers Handbook*. Arlington, VA: NTL Institute.

Maturana, H., & Varela, F. (1980). *Autopoiesis and Cognition*. Dordrecht: Reidel.

Morgan, G. (1986). *Images of Organization*. Newbury, CA: Sage.

Morgan, G. (1988). *Riding the Waves of Change: Developing Managerial Competencies for a Turbulent World*. San Francisco, CA: Jossey-Bass.

O'Hanlon, W. H. (1987). *Tap Roots: Underlying Principles of Milton Erickson's Therapy and Hypnosis*. New York: W. W. Norton.

Ong, W. J. (1982). *Orality and Literacy*. London: Methuen.

Palazzoli, M. S., Boscolo, L., Cecchin, G., & Prata, G. (1970). *Paradox and Counterparadox*. New York: Jason Aronson.

Pearce, W. B. (1993). *Remarks at the KCC Summer Conference. Co-creating the Future of Systemic Management and Consultation*.

Penn, P., & Sheinberg, M. (1986). A systemic model for consultation. In: L. Wynne, S. McDaniel, & T. Weber (Eds.), *The Family Therapist as Systems Consultant*. New York: Guilford Press.

Potter, J., & Wetherell, M. (1987). *Discourse and Social Psychology*. Newbury, CA: Sage.

Rackham, N. (1987). *Making Major Sales*. Aldershot: Gower.

Reason, P. (Ed.) (1988). *Human Inquiry in Action*. Newbury, CA: Sage.

Reason, P., & Rowan, J. (1981). *Human Inquiry*. New York: Wiley.

Reed, B. (1976). Organization role analysis. In: C. L. Cooper (Ed.), *Developing Social Skills in Managers*. New York: Macmillan.

Schein, E. (1987). *Process Consultation, Vol. 2*. Reading, MA: Addison-Wesley.

Senge, P. (1990). *The Fifth Discipline*. New York: Doubleday.

Sheridan, A. (1980). *Foucault: The Will to Truth*. London: Tavistock.

Shotter, J., & Gergen, K. (Eds.) (1989). *Texts of Identity*. London: Sage.

Sinclair, J. (1992). *An ABC of NCP*. London: Aspen.

Von Bertalanffy, L. (1956). General Systems Theory. *General Systems, 1*: 1–10.

Von Foerster, H. (1981). *Observing Systems*. Seaside, CA: Intersystems Publications.

Von Glasersfeld, E. (1984). An introduction to radical constructionism. In: P. Watzlawick (Ed.), *The Invented Reality*. New York: W. W. Norton.

Walsh, K., & Davis, H. (1993). *Competition and Services, The Impact of the Local Government Act, 1988*. London: H.M.S.O.

Watzlawick, P. (1976). *How Real Is Real?* New York: Random House.

Watzlawick, P., Beavin, J., & Jackson, D. (1967). *Pragmatics of Human Communication*. New York: W. W. Norton.

Watzlawick, P., Weakland, J., & Fisch, R. (1974). *Change*. New York: W. W. Norton.

Weick, K. E. (1979). *The Social Psychology of Organizing*. Reading, MA: Addison-Wesley.

Weisbord, M. R. (1990). *Productive Workplaces*. San Francisco, CA: Jossey-Bass.

White, M. (1991). *Deconstruction and Therapy*. Dulwich Centre Newsletter, No. 3.

Wittgenstein, L. (1958). *Philosophical Investigations*. Oxford: Basil Blackwell.

INDEX

strategies, level of, of constructionist
consulting, 128–130
structural therapy, 170, 171
definition, 194
structure-determined change, 86, 156,
168
definition, 194
structured discussion, 97
structures:
dissipative, definition, 190
organization, hierarchy, power,
and control in, 38
symmetrical relationship, 152
definition, 194
system:
complex, change in, 84–102
observing, 31, 126, 131, 139, 161
vs. observed, 13
problem-determined, 13, 88, 118,
132, 133, 142, 161
sculpt, 70, 71
-wide dialogue, facilitating, 142–
143
systemic, 3
definition, 2
systemic family therapy, 175
systemic hypothesis, 26, 83, 117, 175,
194, 195
systemic questioning, 26
systemic thinking, 21, 119, 171, 175,
187
and cause and effect, 11–13
and change, 22
concepts of, 3
and constructed realities, 18
constructionist, 2
focus of, on context, 15
vs. good organizational common
sense, 13
key concepts of, 9–10
and language, 18
and meanings, 16–17
and observation of organizations,
12
and observer situation, 20
origins of, 3
and parts of system, 24
and reframing, 4
and team discussions, 19
use of, to plan and design strategic
and development event, 61

system, observed, vs. observing, 31–
35
systemic/social constructionist,
124

Tavistock Clinic, 174, 176
Taylor, F., 35
team:
mind, 19
reflecting, 19
thinking, 19–20
television, 52
therapy:
strategic, 170
definition, 194
structural, 170, 171
definition, 194
thinking:
contingency, 82
linear, 12, 114, 132
positivist, 31
strategic, 139
team, 19–20
tight feedback, 14
training:
cascade, 42, 48, 143
interactive vs. instructive, 47–48
Trist, E. L., 36, 172

universal solutions, 29, 192
definition, 195

values, level of, of constructionist
consulting, 127–128
Varela, F., 19
Von Bertalanffy, L., 9, 10
Von Foerster, H., 13
Von Glasersfeld, E., 18

Walsh, K., 46
Watzlawick, P., 3, 52, 121, 192
Weakland, J., 3
Weick, K. E., 53
Weisbord, M. R., 36, 142
Wetherell, M., 19
White, M., 31, 135
Winderman, L., 13
Wittgenstein, L., 59, 136, 190
working hypotheses, 26, 72, 81,
194
definition, 195